Lewis Boss

A Statement in Respect to the United States

Naval Observatory and its Organization

Lewis Boss

A Statement in Respect to the United States
Naval Observatory and its Organization

ISBN/EAN: 9783744742870

Printed in Europe, USA, Canada, Australia, Japan

Cover: Foto ©Suzi / pixelio.de

More available books at **www.hansebooks.com**

A STATEMENT

IN RESPECT TO THE

United States Naval Observatory

AND

ITS ORGANIZATION.

PREPARED BY

LEWIS BOSS,

Director of Dudley Observatory, Albany, N. Y.

1891.

ALBANY :
CHAS. VAN BENTHUYSEN & SONS,
1891.

This Statement in reference to the Naval Observatory was prepared some months ago, substantially in its present form. Its length seemed to render publication inadvisable ; and it was not originally intended for that purpose. The illegibility of the manuscript copies, together with expressions of opinion from friends that a somewhat detailed statement of the principles and evidence upon which astronomers base. their views in regard to this question might find some readers who would deem it more satisfactory than a mere dogmatic summary, has led the author to submit this document for publication. This he has been able to do through the voluntary contributions of American astronomers, to whom his acknowledgments are due.

At the same time—and while the author is indebted to astronomers for many valuable suggestions—he, alone, is responsible for any errors of fact or opinion which this Statement may contain.

Albany, N. Y., December, 1891.

TABLE OF CONTENTS.

Within the past decade the Government of the United States has been making provision for an astronomical observatory, which in cost is scarcely to be surpassed anywhere in the world. Not including some minor items, the appropriations for this purpose thus far made are:

For purchase of site....................................	$75,000 00
For construction of principal buildings...............	400,000 00
For other constructions, alteration, repair and remounting of instruments, removal, etc.........	136,689 00

Total for the new Naval Observatory...... $611,689 00

In addition to these sums, the Naval Observatory was already in possession of instruments, books and furniture, the original cost of which was not less than $100,000. The great equatorial telescope cost $50,000, less than twenty years ago. The real value of all this apparatus for the purpose of removal to the new observatory cannot be regarded as less than $50,000. This brings up the cost of the new Naval Observatory to not less than $650,000. But when the current appropriation of $136,689 shall have been exhausted, the new observatory cannot by any means be regarded as completely equipped. Taking as a basis the estimate of $294,487.20, officially submitted to Congress at its last session (51st Cong., 2d session, H. R. Ex. Doc., Nos. 79 and 147), about $160,000 more will be needed to carry out the plans which have been made. This would raise the total cost of the plant for the new Naval Observatory to more than $800,000.

The sum already appropriated is larger than that which has been devoted to a like purpose for any national observatory in the world. The Russian Imperial Observatory at Pulkowa, has always, heretofore, been regarded as the most remarkable example of the generosity of governments toward astronomy. It has an equipment of unexampled perfection, and is provided with quarters for all the employees. The original cost in 1845 was 2,100,000 paper roubles, usually estimated to be about equivalent to $340,000. Extraordinary additions to the equipment in recent years, including the astro-physical laboratory, as well as the thirty-inch telescope, the largest, or most powerful, in possession of any national observatory, may possibly have added $200,000 to the cost of plant.

The cost of the new Naval Observatory is large enough to have built, equipped, and to have furnished funds for the perpetual endowment of two such institutions as the Bonn Observatory, renowned for the great number and lasting value of its contributions to astronomical science throughout the past fifty years. Obviously the people of the United

States are justified in anticipating important results to follow this large expenditure.

But it is not simply in relation to the new observatory that Congress has shown its liberality. If we include extraordinary expenditures, more than $2,000,000 have been appropriated for the benefit of the Observatory during the past twenty-five years. Excluding these, there has been expended for current maintenance of the Naval Observatory, an average of $56,000 annually, during the same period. (Appended note B.) With two or three exceptions, this sum is very much greater than has ever been devoted to the like maintenance of any other observatory in the world. Even excluding the salaries of the superintendent and other line officers of the Navy, the annual expenditure has averaged very nearly $41,000. (Appended note B.) The respective amounts for the present fiscal year are materially greater than these averages.

Large as these sums are, they are deemed inadequate for the future. In his annual report for the year ending June 30, 1890, the Superintendent says:

"It is scarcely necessary to add that, when the new Naval Observatory is completed and equipped, the force of astronomers and assistant astronomers will have to be materially increased if the observatory is to be worthy of our great and progressive country."

These expenditures very naturally invite the careful scrutiny of those who are conversant with the history and present state of astronomy; they must sooner or later attract the serious attention of Congress; and they warrant the inquiry, in behalf of the people of the United States, by those who are capable of judging of the answer, as to what precautions have been and are to be taken to secure a return in results corresponding in importance to this more than imperial munificence. If the money has been judiciously and economically expended; if there is promise of adequate scientific return, and if the nation can justly be proud of its observatory, it is not likely that the people will seriously object to this large expenditure. It is consonant with the growing preëminence of our country in wealth and power, to desire to have the best equipped and most useful observatory in the world.

What object is this expenditure designed to subserve? Is the whole, or any great part of it necessary in relation to the practical operation of the Navy? If it is, then the propriety of a naval administration for it is more easily understood. It will be shown, however, that there is absolutely no excuse for more than a small fraction of the appropriations which have been made for the Naval Observatory, if practical service to the Navy is alone considered; that such an establishment as this has been, and as the new observatory is evidently designed to be, is not needed by the Navy; and that naval officers in common with astronomers, have regarded it as an institution maintained to promote the national interest in astronomical investigation. Supposing the latter view to be correct, it is possible that a question may arise as to the best form of administration for a national observatory which is essentially astronomical. It might be supposed at first sight that nothing could be more natural than that an astronomer should be chosen to manage an astronomical observatory. Perhaps the majority of people, left to their own common sense view of the subject, would resent the idea that there could be two opinions about it, and would look with some degree of impatience upon a formal argument to prove that an astronomer ought to be selected for the chief direction of astronomical work, as too much like an attempt to prove an axiom. This is an embarrassment which the advocates of reform in the administration of the Naval Observatory have to encounter. Yet it appears to be necessary, since the authorities of Government have practically endorsed the opposite view, though there is no evidence that the merits of the question have heretofore received, either from Congress or from executive authority, the attention which its importance demands.* The Superintendent of the Naval Observatory has always been a line officer of the Navy. It has been held by officers of the Navy on duty at the Observatory—though probably not by naval officers at large — that they can conduct its affairs with more propriety and efficiency than would be possible were the chief control exercised by a civilian astronomer. On the other hand, astronomers maintain that the Government observatory should be placed in charge of an astronomer; that the conduct of a government observatory by a man who is not an astronomer of experience is an anomaly without relevant precedent in the history of astronomy; that it has no warrant in a discussion of the abstract principles which apply to the case; and that it finds no justification in the results which have actually been produced under this form of administration by the Naval Observatory itself. Naval officers at the Observatory have hitherto ignored the force of universal precedent, as they may do if they have succeeded in establishing another of greater weight; they contest the argument from abstract principles; they have declared at various times that scientific results fully justify the form of administration adopted for the Naval Observatory.

THE FUNCTION OF A NATIONAL OBSERVATORY.

It would be idle at this late day to urge the support of national observatories on the ground of practical utility alone. Their practical utility is great, but it is secondary and incidental. The time has come

---

* Since this was written, Hon. Benjamin F. Tracy, Secretary of the Navy, in his annual report for 1891, has recommended to Congress "the adoption of legislation which shall enable the President to appoint, at a sufficient salary, without restriction, from persons either within or outside of the naval service, the ablest and most accomplished astronomer who can be found for the position of Superintendent" of the Naval Observatory at Washington

when national observatories must rely for support almost wholly upon the more powerful argument of scientific utility. It does happen that there are departments of astronomy which have an important relation to commercial utility. Even in respect to them, at the present day, the necessity for the great labor and refinement which is practiced upon them arises almost wholly from theoretical and scientific needs, rather than from those which are purely practical; and at the same time, unless this refinement of methods and work is practiced at any given observatory, its results will possess no value in comparison with those which are elsewhere produced.

There are also other important fields of astronomical investigation, which do not pretend to minister to the merely physical needs of mankind, but which must, nevertheless, usually be cared for by governments. To provide for that class of astronomical researches, wherein constantly recurring operations must be faithfully maintained, year after year, for centuries, perhaps, and in which definite deductions can be reached only through the accumulation of a great multitude of identical or similar measurements and calculations, where the interest must be maintained at high tension through years of toil—often extending beyond the lifetime of a single individual,—this is the work of a national observatory; it is the world's work and must be done. Ultimately, these departments of astronomical research yield the most comprehensive and impressive truths known to science. Individual workers in astronomy having small means usually prefer to engage in work where the attainment of a definite result is not too much imperilled by the accidents always possible to an individual life. They must also confine themselves to undertakings which there is a reasonable prospect of carrying out with limited assistance. National observatories are not maintained altogether to serve the personal tastes of individual astronomers. They are public institutions, subject to public criticism as well as to praise, and established to satisfy the most general demands of the world for astronomical information of indispensable general interest in departments not likely to receive adequate attention at private observatories.

Hence the directors of nearly all great national observatories are required to report their proceedings to a board of visitors, or commission of astronomers, whose business it is to see that the observatory subject to their inspection is properly and efficiently meeting a public demand. In this as in other matters it is the function of Government to do for the people what ought to be done, and what the people cannot so well do for themselves in their unorganized capacity. This claim for astronomy has been advocated by great statesmen in all times; and it is now practically acknowledged by every civilized government in the world.

Well understanding these facts, the friends of astronomy in this country have always been solicitous for the proper conduct of the only astronomical observatory which is supported by our Government. They believe that its most important function is discharged when it sustains and enlarges the intellectual dignity and prestige of the nation. They believe that Americans are at least the equals of any other nationality in the natural capacity for successful scientific investigation. The observatory supported by the Government must stand before the world as largely representing American astronomy. Astronomers, therefore, consider it an entirely warrantable exercise of the privileges of citizenship, when they respectfully urge that the authorities of Government give serious and immediate attention to the question whether an establishment, such as the Naval Observatory aims to be, is more properly directed through military organization under the superintendence of a naval officer, than it is likely to be under a civilian organization with direction by an astronomer.

The construction of a new observatory, on an unexampled scale of expenditure renders the present a peculiarly appropriate time for an impartial examination of this question by those with whom the decision must rest.

The statement which follows is designed to present the claims of American astronomers in relation to the administration of the Government observatory through arguments based upon competent evidence. To a great extent this evidence can be drawn from official sources. In regard to the statements of scientific facts and opinions, it is believed that every one of them is susceptible of verification by the published records, and by the united testimony of the most competent astronomers.

SECTION I.—Opinions of Public Men During the First Half of this Century in Reference to a Government Observatory.

It becomes necessary to look somewhat carefully into the origin of the Naval Observatory; since this origin is often cited in defense of the present system. It is necessary to determine, first, what sort of an institution the early advocates of a national observatory for this country intended, and, secondly, whether or not, Congress with due deliberation placed an astronomical observatory in the hands of naval officers.

The Naval Observatory derived its existence from the law of 1842, which authorized the construction of a new building termed the " Depot of Charts and Instruments." The public documents contain much evidence that the establishment of a national observatory had been favorably considered by executive authority and by committees of Congress at various times in the early history of the country.* A few citations will suffice to illustrate the character of the whole.

---

* The late Professor Nourse, U. S. N., in his " Memoir of the Founding and Progress of the United States Naval Observatory " (Washington Astronomical Observations for 1871, Appendix IV.) has collated citations upon this subject from the public documents of that period.

During the administration of President Madison, the establishment of a first meridian and of an astronomical observatory was advocated. The question had been referred to Mr. Monroe, Secretary of State, for an opinion. He reported, July 3, 1812, advocating the proposition and emphasizing the advantages to science. Among other things in reference to a first meridian for America, he said :

"For this purpose an observatory would be of essential utility. It is only in such an institution, to be founded by the public, that all the necessary implements are likely to be collected together ; that systematic observations can be made for any length of time ; and that the public can be made secure of the results of the labors of scientific men. In favor of such an institution, it is sufficient to remark that every nation which has established a first meridian has also established an observatory." (Am. Misc. State Papers, Vol. II., p. 194.)

The committee of Congress to which this was referred, of which Hon. S. L. Mitchell was chairman and Hon. John C. Calhoun a member, reported on Jan. 20, 1813, a bill for a national observatory, and in support of it said among other things :

"The most ready way of obtaining the information they desired, from noting the phenomena of the heavens, is by the establishment of an observatory. This may be erected at the city of Washington. By such an institution, means may be adopted, not only to fix the first meridian, but to ascertain a great number of other astronomical facts and occurrences through the vigilance of a complete astronomer." (Am. Misc. State Papers, Vol. II., p. 197.)

This is the idea of a true national observatory in a nut-shell. A memorial from Mr. William Lambert, an amateur astronomer of great ability who had been employing his leisure to determine the longitude of the Capitol, was the occasion of these reports. At a later date, Feb. 25, 1824, President Monroe transmitted to Congress another and more elaborate memorial by Mr. Lambert, who had meanwhile resigned from the Pension Office, to be employed on this longitude work for the Government.

In his first message to Congress, in 1825, President John Quincy Adams urged the establishment of a national observatory in these words :

"Connected with the establishment of a university, or separate from it, might be undertaken the erection of an astronomical observatory, with provision for the support of an astronomer, to be in constant attendance on the phenomena of the heavens, and for the periodical publication of his observations. It is with no feeling of pride as an American, that the remark may be made, that, on the comparatively small territorial surface of Europe, there are existing more than one hundred and thirty of these light-houses of the skies ; while throughout the whole American hemisphere there is not one. If we reflect a moment upon the discoveries which in the last four centuries have been made in the physical constitution of the universe by means of these buildings and of observers stationed in them, shall we doubt of their usefulness to every nation ? And while scarcely a year passes over our heads without bringing some new astronomical discovery to light, which we must fain receive at second hand from Europe, are we not cutting ourselves off from the means of returning light for light, while we have neither observatory nor observer upon our half of the globe, and the earth revolves in perpetual darkness to our unsearching eyes ?"

The select committee, to which this recommendation was referred, offered a bill "to establish an observatory in the District of Columbia," and in support of it adopted a report prepared by General Macomb, Chief of Engineers, in which occurs the following :

"The astronomer ought to be independent in the performance of his duties, but accountable for the results, for his industry, and the correctness of his observations and calculations. The results of his scientific labors should be given to the world, in order that they might be duly examined by astronomers of different countries. * * * Foreign as well as domestic criticism would thus stimulate the astronomer to greater vigilance and attention. * * * As an astronomer with the requisite talents and qualifications would be obliged to devote all his time and attention to the duties of his station, it is not to be expected that a fit person could be procured for this situation without the compensation of a liberal salary." (H. R., Report No. 124, 19th Cong., 1st session.)

The committee, through the report of General Macomb, also recommends that, " as soon as circumstances would permit, a nautical almanac, or astronomical ephemeris should be prepared and published for the use of the Navy and commercial marine."

The Secretary of the Navy, on March 18, 1830, in reply to a letter from the chairman of the House Committee on Naval Affairs wrote:

"As far as I have been able to obtain information on the subject, an astronomical observatory would be a desirable establishment in the United States for the following reasons :

1st. In a national point of view, as it would furnish the means of making such observations as would enable astronomers to ascertain or calculate the positions of the heavenly bodies at any time without being dependent on other nations for the same ; and would be, moreover, a fixed point to whose meridian (commonly called a first meridian when used for geographical purposes) terrestrial objects may, with certainty, be referred, as far as respects their longitudes.

2d. It would, furthermore, be desirable in a scientific point of view, as it would present the means of comparing certain astronomical results, for the purpose of determining the figure of the earth and improving theories relative to the motions of the planetary bodies.' (Nourse, " Memoir on the Founding," etc., p. 12.)

In this communication the practical side of the scientific duties of a Government observatory are outlined.

John Quincy Adams, chairman of a select committee of the House of Representatives, in his second report on the Smithson Fund, March 5, 1840, says :

"The express object of an observatory is the increase of knowledge by new discovery. * * * There is no richer field of science opened to the exploration of man in search of knowledge than astronomical observation ; nor is there, in the opinion of this committee, any duty more impressively incumbent on all human governments than that of furnishing means, and facilities, and rewards, to those who devote the labors of their lives to the indefatigable industry, the unceasing vigilance, and the bright intelligence indispensable to success in these pursuits. (H. R. Report, No. 277, 27th Cong., 1st session.)

In 1842, Mr. Adams reiterated his views in support of the establishment of a national observatory in his third report on the Smithson Fund, together with a bill for that purpose. (H. R. Rep. No. 587, bill 386; 27th Cong., 2d session.) Notwithstanding the bitter political animosities of the time, the influence of Mr. Adams (most vigorously exerted in 1826, 1838, 1840, 1842 and 1844) contributed more than any other to prepare official sentiment for the establishment of an astronomical observatory by the Government. This fact is clearly recognized by Lieut. M. F. Maury, the first Superintendent of the Naval Observatory, in a letter to Mr. Adams, dated Nov. 17, 1847. Lieutenant Maury says :

" Your efforts to advance in America the cause of practical astronomy are known to the world. The lively interest which you continue to manifest in all that concerns the observatory, causes you to be considered as one of its most active and zealous friends. It is proud of the relation. * * * As a subject for congratulation with one who has borne so conspicuous a part in establishing a Naval and National Observatory in this country, permit me to call your attention," etc. (Southern Literary Messenger, Vol. XIV., p. 4.)

At the same time it must be borne in mind that so late as June, 1844, when the buildings and instruments of the Naval Observatory were nearly ready for use, Mr. Adams did not then consider the new "House for the Depot of Charts" as suited to fulfil the object which he and other friends of a national astronomical observatory had in view; for, on June 7, 1844, as chairman of a select committee, in a report on the disposition of the Smithson funds, accompanied with a bill, the establishment of a national observatory was specified as one of the objects to be provided for from the funds arising from the Smithson bequest. It was recommended that the accumulated interest, $300,000, be set apart for building, equipment and endowment. He was not then aware of the extent to which a simple bill to provide a house for the depot might be construed as conferring authority for the establishment of one of the most lavishly supported astronomical institutions of modern times.

SECTION II.—The Origin of the Naval Observatory.

The history of the immediate official acts which led to the organization of the Naval Observatory can be related in a brief space. Since 1830, the Navy had occupied a small rented house in Washington as a depot of charts,—that is to say, a place in which maps, charts, chronometers and other nautical appliances could be stored and from which, from time to time, they could be issued as needed. Connected with the house was a small temporary structure, or observing room, which served the purpose of sheltering some unimportant astronomical instruments that were chiefly employed for the purpose of rating the chronometers. These in the year 1837 were placed in charge of Lieutenant Gilliss, who immediately developed an interest in astronomical pursuits, for which the observations, deemed advisable to be made in connection with the exploring expedition of Lieutenant Wilkes in 1838 and subsequent years, afforded a welcome opportunity. Lieutenant Gilliss proved to be a remarkably assiduous observer who, in his scientific enthusiasm, accomplished far more than was called for by the letter of his instructions. With time and practice he gained facility in the use of the simple instruments at his command, and, no doubt, it is chiefly to his influence that the. plan for what was to become a Naval Observatory was proposed and executed. In his Annual Report for 1841, the Secretary of the Navy, acting upon the report of the Navy Commissioners as to the inadequacy of the then existing office for charts and instruments, said :

" Permit me to express my entire approval of the suggestion of the Commissioners, in relation to a suitable depot of charts and instruments belonging to the Navy. These have been procured at great labor and expense, and are indispensable in the naval service. The small expenditure which will be necessary to preserve them in a condition, always ready for use, is not worth a moment's consideration when compared with the great purposes they are designed to answer. They are a necessary part of a naval establishment worthy of the present and growing greatness of our country." (Ex. Doc., 27th Cong., 2d, session, Vol. 1, p. 367.)

It appears likely from the interesting report of Lieutenant Gilliss of February 7, 1845 (Senate Doc., No. 114 ; 28th Cong., 2d session), that not much attention would have been paid to this proposal but for the personal exertions with members of both Houses of Congress by Lieutenant Gilliss himself. The bill which finally passed on the last day of the session (approved August 31, 1842), reads :

"An act to authorize the construction of a depot of charts and instruments of the Navy of the United States. *Be it enacted*," etc.

" That the Secretary of the Navy be, and he is hereby, authorized to contract for the building of a suitable house for a depot of charts and instruments of the Navy of the United States, on a plan not exceeding in cost twenty-five thousand dollars." [Section 2 appropriates $10,000 for the purposes of this act, and section 3 makes provisions for the site.]

Under the provisions of this law, Lieutenant Gilliss, acting under the orders of the Secretary of the Navy, proceeded to construct and equip the present Naval Observatory.

This was not quite all. The bill which was introduced in the House, March 15, 1842, and which was identical in terms with the Senate bill that finally became a law, was accompanied with a report by the Committee on Naval Affairs, Hon. Francis Mallory, chairman. (H. R. No. 449; 27th Cong., 2d session. See also appended Note A.)

Mr. Mallory appears to have warmly espoused the cause which Lieutenant Gilliss was advocating, and devotes some paragraphs of his report to consideration of astronomical needs. (Appended Note A.) "A small observatory is absolutely essential to the depot," he says, " without it the duties cannot be performed." This statement, together with other comments by Mr. Mallory, favorable to the idea that astronomical work should be carried on by the Navy, appears to have been considered sufficient authorization for the construction of an observatory on a large scale for the Navy.

In his report of 1845 previously cited, Lieutenant Gilliss says :

"Taking the report of the naval committee which accompanied the bill (See Report No. 449, House of Representatives, session 1841-2) as the exponent of the will of Congress, the honorable Secretary of the Navy directed me, on the 9th September, 1842, to visit the principal Northern cities, for the purpose of obtaining information respecting a plan, which, whilst it combined essentials should not exceed in cost the appropriated sum."

That the Navy Department, though without express authority, definitely intended to establish an astronomical observatory, as distinguished from such an observatory as it had in connection with the old depot, may be perceived, not only from the character of new equipment provided after prolonged journeyings and numerous consultations with American and European astronomers by Lieutenant Gilliss, but also from the following paragraphs, among others, in the aforesaid report:

"Much interest was evinced in the success of the Naval Observatory by the distinguished *savans* I had the honor to meet; and, in token of their gratification at the establishment of an institution by the United States, where science will be prosecuted, they have contributed to its library the following books.   *   *   *

"In the mere store rooms for the charts and instruments, or depot, as it is called, I feel no anxiety. The house on Capitol Hill would have answered quite as well as any other [up to 1842, Gilliss had been superintendent of that establishment], and a three and a half feet transit, in a box ten feet square, would have served to obtain the time for the comparing clock. These, therefore, possessed no attractions for me, and I should have regarded it as time misspent to labor so earnestly, only to establish a depot. My aim was higher. It was to place an institution under the management of *naval officers*, where, in the practical pursuit of the highest known branch of science, they would compel an acknowledgment of abilities hitherto withheld from the service."

That the new observatory should have a naval organization rests on better authority than that for founding an observatory. Evidently a new " house for a depot of charts " was intended for the Navy. Furthermore, in the report of Mr. Mallory, are found opinions of the committee as to the manner in which astronomical and meteorological observations can best be conducted.

" If officers can be found with taste for such duties," says the committee, "an observatory will give more information to the world under a military organization, in one year, than under any other direction in two." * * * * "Night watching in stormy weather finds few followers and we can only hope to obtain the desired information [in meteorology] when those engaged in its pursuit have *duty* to compel a flagging inclination." (More fully in appended Note A).

These views undoubtedly indicate that in the judgment of the committee, our naval officers, if given the opportunity, would far outstrip the astronomers of the old world in the amount and value of scientific work to be produced.

Hitherto, there has been a tradition that, when the question of future management of the observatory, which had grown upon its hands and was about ready for use, came up for consideration, the Navy Department grew to distrust the idea of placing a naval officer in charge. It had begun to suspect that an observatory is an institution where the duties are extremely technical. Moreover, bills for the establishment of a national observatory, had been offered in Congress on several previous occasions, and now when the new depot was nearly ready for occupancy another bill for this purpose was pending. It may be inferred that the few practical astronomers of the country, in ignorance, possibly, of the extent to which the Navy would be able to develop the purposes of legislation, were interesting themselves in this bill. It might not have been difficult to suppose there was some chance that this bill would pass. Nothing would then have been more natural than that the naval authorities, wishing the credit for inaugurating such an institution to inhere in their own department, should have thought it best to appoint a civilian as chief astronomer, or to make some other compromise. It appears that Lieutenant Maury, who was then in charge of the old depot, had become aware of the discussion in the department, and was not satisfied with the course things were taking. In a letter, of Jan. 1, 1847, addressed to his intimate friend, William Blackford, Esq., of Lynchburg, Virginia, Lieutenant Maury wrote:

" You know I did not want the place [Superintendent] and only decided to keep it [he had been in charge of the existing depot] when I heard it had been promised to a civilian, under a plea that no one in the Navy was fit for it. I then went to Mason [Secretary of the Navy, and like Maury, a native of Virginia] pronounced *that* the repetition of a practical libel, and told him he must stand by me. He did so, and though I had never seen an instrument of the kind before, and had no one with me who had, I was determined to ask no advice or instruction from the savans." * * * (Life of Matthew Fontaine Maury, compiled by his daughter, Mrs. D. F. M. Corbin, London, 1888.)

Mason "stood by" Maury, and he was placed in charge of the observatory in October, 1844. Mr. Sears C. Walker, one of the ablest practical astronomers then in the country, became his assistant. Professors

Coffin, Hubbard and Keith were also detailed to the observatory in the year, 1845, they holding commissions in the Navy as Professors of Mathematics. Coffin and Hubbard took the laboring oars in the observations; Walker and Coffin became the mainstays in the computations, and in the preparation of them for publication. All were, however, comparatively inexperienced.

Lieutenant Maury was a man of good abilities. He was also of a restless and enterprising spirit. He was possessed of great fertility of invention and resource. He had suffered from a serious accident, which had incapacitated him for active service in his profession. The possibility of his enforced retirement from the service, hung over him as a standing menace, and actually threatened in 1859. The problem of future employment, commensurate with his ambitious energy of mind, was one that occupied his thoughts and found expression in communications to his friends during this period. Had the tide of circumstances set in the proper direction, and had not law and immemorial custom protected certain professional employments against inexperience far more securely than astronomical and scientific appointments in this country have ever been guarded, it is easy to imagine that Lieutenant Maury might have accepted the office of judge in a higher court, or of chief surgeon in a hospital, with the same intrepid self-reliance, which he evinced in assuming the superintendence of the United States Naval Observatory.

To prevent this, there was no authoritative voice in science, no recognized body of astronomers, around which awakened public sentiment could gather for leadership. The idea of a Government astronomical observatory was, therefore, launched on a sea of inexperience, where it long drifted, the sport of the winds of misconception and waves of prejudice. By the merest chance it was seized upon as derelict by the Navy and brought to a strange port. There it was libeled without chance for a hearing; and there it has remained in an unseaworthy condition ever since.

It will subsequently appear that the vague astronomical references in Mr. Mallory's committee report (see appended Note A) must be regarded, from the naval point of view, as not only authorizing the kind of observations which formerly occupied the Greenwich Observatory—the observation of sun, moon, planets, and principal fixed stars,—but also much more. From the first, and throughout its history, the Naval Observatory has not hesitated to undertake any sort of astronomical observations permissible to its equipment and men. Such have been the observations of telescopic planets (or asteroids), planetary moons (or satellites), comets, double stars, telescopic stars, and nebulas, though none of all these can even be seen by the mariner at sea—a small percentage of comets excepted. It is for such purposes that the Observatory demands these large appropriations from Congress

SECTION III.—NAVAL AND MARINE OBSERVATORIES IN OTHER COUNTRIES.

It will be in order now to form an opinion in regard to the actual results from management of the Naval Observatory by naval officers. It would scarcely be fair to hold the Navy responsible for the fulfilment of the prediction by 'Mr. Mallory, that an observatory administered by military methods "would accomplish more in one year, than under any other direction in two." Yet the claim of naval officers of the Observatory, that its scientific career has been such as to place it in the front rank among similar institutions of the world, is entitled to candid and impartial consideration.

The task of making a direct comparison of the work of our Naval Observatory with that of other national institutions, to the disadvantage of the former, is not a pleasant one for any right-minded American astronomer. But it must be undertaken.

Officers of the Navy on duty at the Observatory, in their efforts to perpetuate their control of the Naval Observatory against the attacks of astronomers, have laid much stress upon the naval character of the establishment. It will be well, therefore, to find out in the first place, what in other countries is practically considered an observatory suitable for purely marine, or naval purposes. This can be done in a very brief space.

There are a number of so-called "Marine observatories" at various European ports. Among these are the observatories at Wilhelmshaven, Trieste, Nicolaieff, Odessa, Bergen and Liverpool. These are all small affairs employing usually two or three persons at most. They are all under civilian control, and are very little, or not at all known for their contributions to the science of astronomy. Their business is chiefly the rating of chronometers, testing of nautical instruments, and the performance of similar duties. There is also what is termed a *Seewarte* at Hamburg, which is not an observatory proper. It does not attempt astronomical observations. It gives great attention to nautical interests and maintains an interesting museum of nautical appliances. Its organization and direction are civilian.

The "Imperial Chronometric Observatory" at Kiel, Germany, is a naval observatory in charge of a naval officer. There is a hydrographic office and naval observatory at Pola, Austria, in charge of a naval officer with four naval officers as assistants. There is a small observatory connected with the hydrographic office at Genoa, Italy. The French have small naval observatories at Brest, Toulon, Cherbourg and other ports. These are merely branches of the hydrographic office, established under lieutenants of the navy, to distribute charts, rate chronometers, and to perform like duties.

As astronomical observatories proper, all these establishments are virtually unknown. They render practical service to their navies, and so far as readily accessible published records show, they render this service with the aid of two or three assistants at most, and with an equipment of instruments which would be regarded as insignificant in relation to an important astronomical observatory.

Besides these there is a naval observatory at San Fernando, Spain, in connection with the naval institute. This is in charge of a naval officer, and there is a large staff of civilian assistants. The Spanish Nautical Almanac is published from this establishment. But the observatory has no record as an astronomical observatory. The Spanish National Observatory is located at Madrid.

There is a national observatory at Lisbon, Portugal, which is in charge of a naval officer, with a very modest equipment and with very few assistants. No astronomical observations worth mentioning have ever been reported from this observatory, which now appears to be practically dead. The positions of assistants are reported vacant.

These illustrations, which practically cover the entire practice of civilized nations in this respect, serve at least to show that with immaterial exceptions, it has not been thought fit to entrust to naval observatories any functions not connected with the strictly practical purposes of the navy and marine. Astronomers well know that observations made for the purpose of determining the places of sun, moon, planets and stars, though they may be rendered useful in the construction of improved tables for seamen, are primarily intended for theoretical uses, or for *astronomical* almanacs and ephemerides. The necessity for the accurate observation of star-places in practical relations arises almost wholly from the needs of earth measurement and similar *operations on land*. In every case the reaching of requisite accuracy, constitutes these observations as scientific work of a high order. It is a matter demanding an order of professional training and experience not likely to be acquired by those whose duties are mainly of another profession.

Distinction between Marine and Astronomical Observatories.

It is necessary to keep clearly in mind this distinction between an immediately practical marine or naval observatory, and an observatory for purposes of astronomical investigation. It is for the interest of those who wish to keep the observatory under control of line officers of the Navy to render this distinction as nebulous as possible. This has been one important source of their success in the continued usurpation of the Government observatory. There has been current a great deal of misconception, and possibly some humbug, in regard to this matter,—misconception on the part of those who do not personally understand the technical details, and humbug on the part of those who, knowing the facts, aid and abet such misconception. Officers of the Naval Observatory have expressed the opinion that the greater part of its work is of immediate commercial utility. (See Report of the Secretary of the Navy for 1877, p. 316; and elsewhere.) Astronomy of immediate practical value in the art of navigation, embraces such operations as the testing and rating of chronometers, furnishing time to shipping at ports, determinations of longitude on the seacoast, and, of course, the rude observations for obtaining a ship's position at sea. These do not constitute a part of what is called scientific investigation, unless the precision attempted is much greater than the mariner requires.

Certain observations requiring the facilities of a fixed and well equipped observatory are useful to the art of navigation. But so far as the navigator is concerned, nine-tenths of the astronomical observations during the past half century, which some would have us believe are exclusively for the benefit of navigation, might as well have been omitted. The tables of the moon could now be kept up to the required standard of accuracy for the mariner, if observations were made in but one year out of ten ; the sun and planets need to be observed for that purpose, not more than three or four years out of a century; the stars would need such attention not more than one year out of two hundred. It is indispensable, to be sure, that such observations should be made ; but to make them in sufficient quantity for the needs of the mariner would be but a small matter for an astronomer.

As to what arrangements are needed for an observatory of the practical type, the most competent authority which our Navy has produced, Lieutenant Gilliss, said :

" In the mere store rooms for the charts and instruments, or depot, as it is called, I feel no anxiety. The house on Capitol Hill would have answered quite as well as any other, and a three and a half feet transit in a box ten feet square, would have served to obtain the time for the comparing clock." (Report of Lieutenant Gilliss, 1845 ; Senate Doc., No. 114 ; 28th Cong., 2d session.)

If the Naval Observatory still claims to be a practical observatory in the sense that naval observatories elsewhere are, then there is no escape from the conclusion that its management has been outrageously extravagant.

SECTION IV.—NATIONAL ASTRONOMICAL OBSERVATORIES IN OTHER
COUNTRIES.

As will hereafter appear, the Naval Observatory is actually an astronomical observatory and must be compared with national astronomical observatories, among which (and especially with Greenwich) its superintendents, when asking for large appropriations, have always desired it to be classed as shown repeatedly in their reports.

In advocating the removal of the observatory to a new site, Admiral Rodgers, Superintendent, said :

" The observatories of Pulkowa, Greenwich, Washington, etc., are placed together in the first class. * * * It will be seen from the foregoing that the observatory is a great national institution," etc. (Report of the Secretary of the Navy for 1877, p. 319.)

Commodore Belknap, Superintendent, in his Annual Report for 1885, writes:

" From its humble beginning in 1838 it [the Naval Observatory] has grown to be one of the most important astronomical centers in the world."

Other quotations of similar import occur elsewhere in this Statement, and still others may easily be found in the annual reports of the superintendents. It is when help is wanted from Congress that these statements are most freely made ; the "practical" theory is reserved for defense against astronomers, since the inference might naturally be supposed to follow that astronomers can present no legitimate claim to the control of a Naval Observatory proper.

If only those observatories are to be considered which employ a working staff nearly equal to that of the Naval Observatory this comparison would have to be restricted to three establishments. But the comparison should relate to quality and methods as well as to mere bulk.

The Imperial Observatory of Russia, at Pulkowa.

The national observatory which concededly holds the primacy among institutions of this class is the Imperial Observatory at Pulkowa. This observatory was established in 1838, and is, therefore, but slightly older than the Naval Observatory. The primary purpose of the Pulkowa Observatory has been to increase the precision of our knowledge regarding the positions and motions of the principal "fixed stars" and the astronomical constants connected with this field of work. This programme includes meridian observations of a fundamental character and high precision upon the sun, larger planets, and stars ; micrometric observations of standard quality upon the principal binary, or revolving double stars ; labors in the interest of the higher forms of geodesy, or earth-measurement; and a variety of minor operations, too great for enumeration in this place.

The star-observations made at Pulkowa enjoy the confidence of astronomers to a greater extent than any others. They have become the fundamental basis upon which rest the observations in the great "zone" undertaking, which has been successfully carried on during the last twenty years through the coöperation of thirteen university-observatories, located in Germany, Russia, Sweden, Norway, Holland, England, and the United States. This project has for its object the accurate determination of the place of every star in the sky down to those which are no more than one-sixteenth as bright as the faintest visible without a telescope. It has been frequently characterized as the most important astronomical undertaking of the present century ; and the work of the Russian Imperial Observatory has been thus far adopted as the fundamental basis for it. The star-places of the astronomical almanac (*Berliner Jahrbuch*) which is used more than any other by astronomers, rest upon the Pulkowa basis; so that in numerous observatories, in nearly every country, an important class of astronomical measurements, which are constantly being made, take the standards established at Pulkowa as the starting point. Even the star-places of the American almanac, one of the best astronomical almanacs in the world, in one of the coördinates necessarily depend more upon the Pulkowa observations than upon those of the Naval Observatory. It is understood that the United States Coast Survey in its longitude work, which is not anywhere surpassed, reduces everything to the Pulkowa standard, concurring in the practice of European organizations of a similar character, though the Naval Observatory is supposed to exist very largely for the very purpose of furnishing the basis, in part at least, for these and similar operations in this country.

The constants of atmospheric refraction have been determined at Pulkowa with unexampled refinement. The quantities of precession, nutation, and aberration,—constants of almost daily use in the computations at astronomical observatories,—have been determined each more than once, through the labors of the Pulkowa astronomers; and the results deduced there are now employed in numberless computations by nearly every astronomer in the world, including those of the Naval Observatory. They are also extensively used in the calculations of astronomical almanacs.

In determining the distances of the stars (one of the most difficult operations in the entire range of science), in researches of precision upon comets, in investigations upon the planets and their satellites, in spectroscopic researches of the highest precision, and in a multitude of studies in various lines, the work of the Pulkowa Observatory is ranked as standard.

There has never been any material interruption in the scientific activity of this famous institution. Every year offers a full complement of excellent observations. The list of memoirs and shorter contributions to astronomy presents remarkable evidence of the great variety and (to those acquainted with them) value of the work accomplished at the Pulkowa Observatory. From 1838 to 1888, these memoirs and papers number 389, and for the last twenty-five years of the period, 230. (Jubilee Celebration of the Pulkowa Observatory.) The subjoined list illustrates the variety of topics treated:

SUBJECTS.	NUMBER.
Stellar Astronomy	62
Bodies of the Solar System	54
Practical Astronomy	20
Geodesy and Geodetic Astronomy	20
Astro-physics	22
Mathematical and Miscellaneous	52

During the first fifty years of its existence (to 1888), the Pulkowa Observatory was under the superintendence of the Struves, father and son, who are reckoned among the ablest practical astronomers of their times. The success of their respective administrations is attributed in the first place, to their unerring judgment as to the particular kind and degree of scientific capacity of the assistants employed by them ; in the second place, to the wisdom displayed by them in the choice of work to be done ; in the third place, to the stimulus exercised by them through personal participation in the astronomical activities of the institution under their charge ; and in the fourth place, to the rigorous superintendence and scrutiny which they exercised upon all the publications of the observatory.

. The observatory is subject to the scientific supervision of the St. Petersburg Academy of Sciences, by which its directors are nominated.

The annual expenditure in 1845 was $33,588, exclusive of payments to members of the Academy. At the present time the annual expenditure is probably somewhat larger,—the amounts are not stated in the reports of the observatory.

The Pulkowa Observatory has responded vigorously to the demands produced by the remarkable awakening of astronomical interest during the past decade or more.

The Royal Observatory at Greenwich.

The Observatory at Greenwich is the prototype of our Naval Observatory, so far as the functions of either have been expressly or indirectly defined. Though established two hundred years ago expressly for perfecting astronomical tables useful in the art of navigation, and though always subject to the British Admiralty, the Greenwich Observatory has always been placed under the direction of civilian astronomers, aided exclusively by civilian assistants. The warrant of the Astronomer Royal, from Charles II. to the present time, has directed him "to apply himself with the utmost care and diligence to the rectifying the tables of the motions of the heavens and the places of the fixed stars, in order to find out the so much desired longitude at sea for perfecting the art of navigation." Until lately, the Greenwich Observatory has adhered more closely to this programme than has our Naval Observatory. Yet civilian astronomers do the work, and superintend it. The names of Flamsteed, Halley,* Bradley, Maskelyne, Pond and Airy, formerly directors of that observatory, are among the most distinguished in the annals of astronomy. The names of the otherwise distinguished direc-

---

* Halley was given a *pro forma* commission in the Navy in connection with scientific expeditions to the southern hemisphere. As fate would have it, however, none of the few observations which he made while director of the Greenwich Observatory, were considered worth publication, though the record is preserved. He, like Flamsteed, was provided neither with instruments nor assistants. His fame as an astronomer is due to his theoretical investigations.

tors of the Naval Observatory are unknown in astronomy, with two exceptions; and none of them has achieved a distinguished place in that science.

The Greenwich observations of sun, moon, planets and stars are highly esteemed by astronomers for their uniform reliability. Since 1750, they form a continuous series, without material interruption (except during the brief administration of Bliss). Since 1845, when our Naval Observatory began similar observations with a like purpose in view, the output from Greenwich has been full and continuous from year to year.

It has been very truly remarked by high authority that were it necessary to reconstruct the lunar and planetary tables anew, this could be done from the Greenwich observations alone, without material sacrifice of accuracy. Since 1845, six important general catalogues of stars have emanated from the Greenwich Observatory. They enjoy a high reputation for accuracy and general excellence. Many other important astronomical researches have been carried on at the Greenwich Observatory during the period under consideration. Among these should be mentioned the series of spectroscopic measurements of the motions of stars toward or from the earth. These very difficult measures in the newest field of astronomy, have been continued for more than a decade, with extraordinary tenacity of purpose. Elsewhere, no regular work of this kind has been attempted and continued for any great length of time.

The record of occultations of stars by the moon, and of the phenomena of planetary satellites is full and continuous. There was also instituted at Greenwich, about twenty years ago, a series of physical observations of the sun to determine the particulars of change going on upon its surface, and these, with the necessary calculations, have been carried on to the present time with the most perfect regularity and success, every day when the sun has been visible.

The meteorological record, and especially the observations to determine the elements of terrestrial magnetism, together with their changes and fluctuations, form at Greenwich one of the largest and most valuable on these subjects in existence.

The directors of the Greenwich Observatory have also been distinguished for the influence which they have exerted not only in the observatory, but also upon the general progress of astronomy. They have been foremost in the counsels of English astronomy.

One reason for the success of their superintendence has been due to the clearness and steadfastness with which they have recognized the line of work which could most advantageously be prosecuted by the Greenwich Observatory, and the inexorable perseverance with which they have held the observatory to its chosen work. The principal feature of that work in the past, has been one in which one or two large observatories could find constant employment to the high advantage of science. Another reason for this success resides in the close attention which the superintendent of the Greenwich Observatory has always given, even for the smallest details in the organization of work, to the observations, and especially to the computations, as well as to publication. Sir George B. Airy, late Astronomer Royal, says:

"In every transaction in or originating in the observatory, without any exception, the Astronomer Royal alone is responsible to the Government. Even in the case of his absence on leave granted by the Admiralty, it is his duty so to direct the chief assistant by written instructions that as little as possible may be left to his discretion." (Par. 8, "Regulations"; Greenwich Observations for 1873, Appendix.)

The current annual expenditure, until recent years, was about $30,000. (Greenw. Obs., 1873.) More recently this has increased to about $42,000, and this amount will, in all probability, be materially increased in the future. In spite of the extremely conservative traditions of this observatory, it has fully recognized the rapidly expanding claims of modern astronomy by greatly enlarging its sphere of work. It is one of the most progressive institutions in the world in that respect.

The Astronomer Royal reports to a "Board of Visitors," composed of members of the Royal Society, of certain astronomers, and of persons appointed by the Admiralty office.

Observatory at the Cape of Good Hope.

The Royal Observatory at the Cape of Good Hope is in many respects similar to that of Greenwich. In spite of its colonial and isolated position, the special obligation of an observatory located in the southern hemisphere has not been neglected. The results achieved by it are of indispensable importance. In earlier years, the *personnel* of this observatory was very small. It was largely employed upon geodetic (or high surveying) work in South Africa. In recent years, the annual expenditure has been about $30,000 (something like half that for the Naval Observatory), and accordingly the astronomical output has been vastly increased.

Since the founding of the Naval Observatory, three important general catalogues of stars have issued from the Cape Observatory, and another is in course of preparation. There is a good complement of observations upon the bodies of the solar system. During the last ten or twelve years there have been made at this observatory numerous determinations of the distances of stars from the earth, and there has been very remarkable activity in the determination of the distances of small planets to ascertain the sun's parallax. These observations are of the highest class.

Important experiments in astronomical photography have been carried on with success; a photographic survey of the entire southern sky, promising results of the highest value, has been completed, and the results will shortly be ready for publication ; observations for longitude, and for places of comets, with a variety of other investigations, have also been made.

The directors of this observatory have been eminent astronomers ; and their success has been largely due to the enthusiasm engendered among assistants by the personal participation of their chiefs in the observations and calculations of the observatory. In the prefatory remarks to the well-known Cape Catalogue of Stars for 1880, Mr. Stone, at that time director of the observatory at the Cape, says :

" Besides the general organization and arrangement of the work, and the making in each year, sufficient observations to check the instrumental adjustments and the general working of the transit circle, I have made it a rule to throw my personal weight upon any part of the work which, from time to time, appeared to flag. I have thus taken a direct share in the work to an extent which appears somewhat unusual on the part of directors of large observatories. * * * I have spared no personal labor to make the work accurate."

These principles are exemplified in the practice of the present Astronomer Royal at the Cape to a remarkable extent. It is in no small measure due to his personal efforts that the courage of observers in attacking the more severe measurements of astronomy has been revived.

The National Observatory at Paris.

The National Observatory at Paris is one of the most extensively equipped in the world, both as to instruments and *personnel*. Its field of operations has been more varied and miscellaneous than is usually the case with large observatories. Its attention has been largely given, however, to the observation of sun, moon, planets, and telescopic stars. During the directorship of the celebrated LeVerrier, a great part of its resources was also given up to mathematical work, and chiefly to the colossal task of computing tables for all the great planets. His administration, owing to his introduction of " military methods," has been severely, and perhaps justly, criticised by his assistants ; though he was one of the most distinguished and best known astronomers of the present century. Considering this instance to have weight, as militating against the desirability of having an astronomer to manage scientific work, it must still be remembered that this case is entirely isolated, so far as the large national observatories are concerned.

The work of constructing an extensive catalogue of the brighter telescopic stars constitutes a very important contribution of the Paris Observatory. The most extensive charts of the fainter telescopic stars have also been made at that observatory. Much attention has also been given to the invention of new forms of astronomical instruments and of new methods in the use of instruments.

In the course of labors for mapping the faint telescopic stars, the idea of charting them with a much higher degree of accuracy by photography was conceived and practically perfected at this observatory. A plan for charting the entire heavens in this way has been initiated, and its practical organization has been successfully completed under the leadership of the Paris Observatory. The coöperation of nearly every one of the leading governments, except our own, has been assured. The preliminary work is in progress.

The present director of the observatory, Admiral Mouchez, is an officer of the navy, many years ago detached for this duty. He is a member of the French Académy of Sciences, and reports to a council which is under the presidency of M. Faye, one of the most distinguished astronomers of France. The organization of the observatory is in no sense naval, nor are its methods. The vice-director is a civilian astronomer, as at Pulkowa, and so are all the assistants. The appointment of a naval officer to the chief direction is entirely exceptional.

In recent times, the French government has supported, in part, a number of astronomical observatories in various parts of France. These are all under civilian direction, and bid fair to raise the astronomical reputation of France to the first rank.

Observatories Supported by the German Government.

The policy of Germany has not led to the establishment of any one great national observatory, but to the division of its patronage among many. Each of the leading states has its observatory, on a comparatively small scale. The principal of these is the Royal Observatory of Prussia at Berlin, best known through the labors of Encke, one of its distinguished directors. The observatory proper is a small establishment employing only three or four assistants; but it is closely connected in an administrative way, with the Astronomical Almanac office, or computing bureau, the new physical observatory at Potsdam, and other scientific interests cared for by government. The services of the director are in constant requisition by his government in a great variety of scientific employments.

The observatory itself is mainly devoted to the precise observation of small planets and telescopic stars. In combination with the Astronomical Almanac office, it has become the head-quarters in relation to the astronomy of the small planets. From 1825 to 1865 this observatory was under the direction of the renowned astronomer Johann Friedrich Encke. The present incumbent, a pupil and active assistant of Encke for many years, succeeded to the direction in 1865. During the period since that time, the Naval Observatory has had nine different superintendents,—six of them since 1882. It is thus easy to understand why the work of the Berlin Observatory, should have been organized on a more consistent and permanent plan, and why that plan should have been more effectively executed than has been the case with the Washington Observatory. The astro-physical observatory at Potsdam, though less than twenty years old and though it employs but a small staff of assistants, has already become authority in standard measurements involving the use of the spectroscope and photographic processes. Its recent work upon the motion of stars in the line of sight, towards or from the earth, is of a highly original character. It is the most valuable that has been done. Already, most interesting discoveries have originated in that work.

As previously stated, there are a large number of university-observatories in the various states of Germany, which are organized on a modest scale and derive their support from government. Some of these, like that of Königsberg in the period from 1812 to 1849, have fulfilled in a great measure the functions of a national observatory. The example of the Königsberg Observatory is a striking illustration of the relation which skilled direction of an observatory bears to the value as well as to the amount of its product. Its director during the period mentioned was Bessel, generally accounted the ablest observing astronomer of the century. Though he had but two or three assistants, the amount and value of the astronomical work produced at that observatory was scarcely equaled by that of any other observatory in the world. Such is the experience of all observatories, large and small,—the abler the director, in the astronomical sense, the more and better the work,—no matter what the ability of assistants may be.

The splendid new observatory at Strasburg and the famous observatory at Bonn, established in the Prussian dominions; the observatory at Leipsic in Saxony ; and the Royal Observatory of Bavaria near Munich, as well as others of a similar character, furnish valuable illustrations of the great value of skilled astronomical direction for such institutions.

Various National Observatories.

The Austrian government supports a national observatory, splendidly housed and equipped, which, however, employs but a small *personnel*, that is chiefly engaged in observations and calculations upon comets and small planets. At present, a large proportion of the new asteroids announced are discovered here. Its large output of results has been concentrated upon definite objects, pursued with fidelity, under the direction of distinguished astronomers, through many succeeding years.

Holland has a quasi-national observatory at Leyden, with a modest but efficient equipment, where four or five astronomers, all told, are employed. Since it has been raised to its present rank (in 1838) its contributions to astronomy, under highly competent practical astronomers, have been of fundamental importance, particularly in the direction of star-observations.

Belgium has a national observatory with a limited number of assistants.

Its work has been about equally divided between star-observations and researches in climatology. Its directors have been among the ablest astronomers of Belgium. A national observatory of considerable importance is located at the capital of Brazil; and there are also small observatories under state patronage in nearly every capital city of the world, in addition to those already mentioned, all under the direction of practical astronomers, imported, sometimes, in default of suitable material at home.

The Argentine National Observatory, at Cordoba.

There is a national observatory which will have a special interest and pertinence in this comparison of observatories with that of Washington. At Cordoba the national observatory of the Argentine Republic was established in 1870 under 'the superintendence of Dr. B. A. Gould, an American astronomer. The labors of this observatory have been mainly directed to observation of the fixed-stars. During thirteen years, from 1871 to 1884, the average annual expenditure for this observatory was $20,963, or less in American currency. In this period, from 1871 to 1884, in addition to observations of comets and a large amount of pioneer work in celestial photography, the star-observations there made and deduced constitute in extent and value by far the largest contribution in this respect ever made by any one observatory in a like space of time. So far as star-observations are concerned, what the Cordoba Observatory achieved in thirteen years exceeds by far, both in quantity and value, the total output of our Naval Observatory during the forty-seven years of its existence.

The history of this observatory is a remarkable illustration of the value of skilled direction in astronomical work. The assistants, in nearly every case, when they arrived at Cordoba from the United States, were without practical experience in astronomical work, and were trained in their duties at the observatory where they were employed. Yet, with immaterial exceptions, the observations by all the observers are of uniformly good quality, and the computations are a model of thoroughness and accuracy. There is remarkably little evidence of wasted labor. All the work seems to have counted in the attainment of a definite purpose. It is seldom in any observatory that assistants have labored with more zealous energy than has been manifested at the Cordoba Observatory. The director himself participated personally in the observations, and in the most important features of the calculations, and he maintained a constant and critical watch upon them throughout. It may safely be inferred that it was this practice which stimulated the assistants to such unusual energy. The thorough manner in which all parts of the work were coördinated into one homogeneous whole, was accomplished through close and practical supervision by the director in person.

With reduced means (nominally, not less), since 1885, under the superintendence or another American astronomer, Dr. J. M. Thome, the Argentine National Observatory is continuing its astronomical career with great credit to those who perform its labors, and to the government which sustains them.

SECTION V.— THE SCIENTIFIC RECORD OF THE UNITED STATES NAVAL OBSERVATORY.

It will now be in order to examine the astronomical record of the United States Naval Observatory in the light of the standards which have been thus established. The significance of these standards will more fully appear in the course of the actual comparison.

The first Superintendent of the Naval Observatory, Lieut. Matthew Fontaine Maury, entered upon the duties of his office, October 1, 1844. In 1845 the astronomical work was begun, with four astronomical assistants and eleven naval officers. The astronomical work of the astronomers was as good, during the first three or four years, as could fairly have been expected in a country where practical astronomy was in its infancy, and at an institution, the chief of which boasted that he knew nothing of the operations he was expected to direct, and "had never seen an [astronomical] instrument of the kind before." The observations were promptly published at first, but publication soon began to fall in arrears. The observations of 1848 were published only in part in 1856; those of 1849-50, in 1859; and those of 1851-2, not until 1867.

It is generally conceded that the observations of the sun, moon, planets and stars in 1851-2 have little or no value; they have been purposely excluded in investigations where they would have been very useful had they been of the requisite accuracy.

During the years 1853 to 1860, inclusive, no annual report of the astronomical observations has ever appeared, because very few observations of any value were made. However, the work done by civilian assistant Ferguson with the equatorial telescope upon comets and minor planets was of good quality and sufficiently continuous. These observations were published from time to time in journals of astronomy. Another exception should be made in respect to observations of stars made by Professor Yarnall in this period. These are creditable, and were collected in a small volume in 1872.

Two great works had been proposed at or near the inauguration of astronomical work at the Observatory. The first was observation of the brighter stars and of the principal bodies of the solar system with a view to providing data for the construction of a Nautical Almanac in a thoroughly " American " sense. The second work proposed was the observation in zones of all the stars south of the celestial equator (and north, for that matter), that could be seen with the meridian instruments of the Observatory.

In regard to the first proposition, the design is fully and repeatedly expressed in the records of the Navy department. Two quotations will suffice. In his annual report, dated November 25, 1844, Hon. John Y. Mason, Secretary of the Navy, says:

"The instruments purchased have been received and placed in the depot. They are well selected, and may be advantageously employed in the necessary observations, with a view to calculate nautical almanacs. For these we are now indebted to foreign nations. This work may be done by our own naval officers without injury to the service, and at very small expense."

In his report of October 20, 1845, Superintendent Maury says:

"Without the English Nautical Almanac, or the nautical ephemeris of some other European nation, our vessels which are now abroad might not find their way home. This office [depot or Naval Observatory] affords the means of wiping off so much of the reproach as is due to us as a nation on this account, for, with the means already at hand, nearly all the requisite data for a nautical ephemeris of our own are obtainable. With a view of obtaining the requisite data for this purpose, a series of observations for the preliminary determinations has been undertaken, and is now in progress. If we attempt to compute the 'American Nautical Almanac'—and this we can do at no greater expense than we pay the English for computing theirs for us—from our own data, it is highly desirable that the data should be *wholly* American."

"If we borrow one element of the work from foreign observations, it would be more creditable to borrow the whole," * * * etc. (Papers accompanying the report of the Secretary of the Navy for 1845.)

Leaving aside consideration of the cautious and skillful progress from a "depot," toward a full fledged observatory, which is manifest in these extracts, and overlooking the impracticability of the plan suggested by Lieutenant Maury, it may be conceded that the observatory began in the path most appropriate to it. It is sufficient commentary to remark that the observatory pursued the practicable part of this programme in a manner for four or five years; with evidence of fatigue for two or three years longer, and then, apparently tired of it, abandoned it altogether, until the revival of the observatory in 1861. It would be exceedingly difficult to find in the pages of the American Nautical Almanac any evidence that the observations of the Naval Observatory have been considered of more value than those of other observatories in its preparation.

In reference to the second project—the observation of faint stars south of the celestial equator—it must be said that while such work is purely astronomical, and not by any stretch of the imagination germane to nautical or naval needs, its creditable performance would have done very much to establish the astronomical reputation of the Naval Observatory and to justify the expenditures which had been made for it.

These observations were begun in 1846, under authority of an order from the Secretary of the Navy, March 6, 1846. The first Superintendent was loyal to the design of accumulating executive precedents for future reference in case the right to do purely scientific work should be thereafter impugned. In this order Secretary Bancroft said:

" * * * I approve your course in making the series of astronomical observations, more immediately necessary for the preparation of a Nautical Almanac.

"The country expects, also, that the observatory will make adequate contributions to Astronomical Science," etc. (Washington Observations, Vol. I., for 1845; Appendix, p. 38.)

The observations in pursuance of this order were continued for several years by a large force of observers, rarely less than six; but their termination is enveloped in obscurity. In fact, the plan was abandoned. The first publication of a part of the observations, made in 1846, occurred in 1860. The remaining observations, 1846–49, were published in 1869 and 1871, twenty years after the latest of them was made ; and then only in the preliminary form, precedent to the formation of a catalogue for practical use. This catalogue has not yet made its appearance.

Commenting on this work in the North American Review (Vol. 105), in 1867, Professor Newcomb, then on duty at the Naval Observatory, says : "So the entire plan ended in ignominious failure." Professor Asaph Hall, U. S. N., under whose editorship the published volumes of these observations were issued, in the introduction to the final volume, says :

"On account of the inexperience of some of the observers and the lack of good organization these observations contain many errors, and the whole work needs a careful revision." (Washington Observations for 1871, Appendix I, p. VI.)

There is no manner of doubt that the observations are of inferior merit. They are rarely used where other observations of the same stars are to be had, and by some astronomers not at all.

The failure of these observations was not altogether the fault of the assistants. The plan of observations was a bad one, such as no experienced astronomer would have sanctioned. For this plan the Superintendent was necessarily responsible.

In the years from 1849 to 1851 a large part of the region of sky covered by this programme was far more completely attended to by Professor F. W. Argelander, Director of the Bonn Observatory. Argelander made all the observations in person, and with very little assistance otherwise. However humiliating to our national pride it may be, it must be acknowledged that these observations by Argelander, in so short a time and with so little help, are superior to those made at the Naval Observatory in the same region at nearly the same time. The Naval Observatory had also the very marked advantage of a latitude twelve degrees farther south. These observations by Argelander, which form a mere episode in his career, first appeared in catalogue form more than thirty years ago.

Whenever a comet, or one of the minor planets, has appeared in that region of sky, even the observers of the Naval Observatory are accustomed to use these star-observations by Argelander, as the basis of their computations, rather than observations of identically the same stars, made at nearly the same time, from beneath their own roof, and published at large expense by their own Government. This finds an illustration, among many others, in the Washington Observations for 1884. That volume contains a large number of observations of comets and small planets, made by locating, from night to night, their positions upon the face of the sky in relation to the stars near them. In 22 cases the position of the star has been quoted from Argelander,—from the Washington Observations in question, not once ; though it was possible to have done so in a number of cases. These observations of planets were made by Commander Sampson, who certainly will not be accused of a desire to overlook the merits of the work done by the Naval Observatory.

This practically comprises the astronomical history of the Naval Observatory down to 1861. It is true that during the ten years preceding that date, Superintendent Maury carried on an important investigation upon the winds and currents of the ocean. But this is no part of the work of an observatory. For this purpose, the costly instruments were of no use whatever. Nor was it necessary to have a force of civilian astronomical assistants to aid him in this work. This was, indeed, practical nautical work germane to a "depot of charts," or a "Hydrographical office," into which the Naval Observatory had become partially reconverted. At any rate the Naval Observatory during that period was no longer fulfilling the mission which the Navy itself had chosen and proclaimed to the world as its vocation. Congress and the people have no guaranty that the management of the Naval Observatory may not at any time, when the fancy seizes it, take up some other line of work and abandon astronomy as it did once before. There is no law in the way, and precedent is in favor of it.

Revival of Astronomical Activity at the Naval Observatory in 1861.

In 1861, after the appointment of Captain Gilliss to the superintendency of the Naval Observatory, it resumed its character as an astronomical institution, though it was still charged with the custody of charts until 1866. After the latter date its duties became quite as purely astronomical as are those of the great national observatories in other lands. Captain Gilliss, though not a thoroughly trained astronomer, was probably more competent for his post than any other superintendent the Observatory has ever had. As an astronomer he was self-taught. In his personal work in astronomy he has not left any very effectual mark on the progress of investigation; yet the same may be said of many professional astronomers who have enjoyed a respectable rank. Captain Gilliss had the temperament of an astronomer. He was earnest and zealous for astronomical progress and appreciated its importance. He displayed good judgment in gathering about him a corps of young assistants of rare scientific promise, some of whom have since demonstrated the wisdom of his choice in a remarkable degree.

In spite of the troubled times, the Naval Observatory now entered upon a career of astronomical activity which was comparatively creditable. Observations of the principal stars and of bodies of the solar system were resumed and have been carried on with unimportant interruptions ever since. At first the old instruments were used. These were already antiquated when they were set up in 1844. Later, a new instrument (Transit Circle) was provided for these observations. Yet the new instrument has not seemed to furnish results equal in value to those obtained with the old instruments. Writing in 1867 of the observations made by the aid of this new instrument, the professor in charge of it says: "Some partial publications of its asteroid observations have appeared in the *Astronomische Nachrichten*, and these show much better for the optical power of the instrument than for its precision." (N. A. Rev., Vol. 105.) The same writer, Professor Newcomb, summing up the work of the observatory up to that time (1867), in this same article says:

"Our judgment of the past work of the Naval Observatory may be summed up thus. That of the first four years, and of the last four years, so far as published, is highly creditable to the country, and to the Navy, all things considered. Among the things to be taken into account are the want of educated astronomers in the beginning and the inferior character of many of the instruments throughout the history of the observatory. During the intervening years [12 years] the operations are creditable to no one but the one or two astronomers by whom all the observations of value were made."

That is to say, the most prominent astronomer at the Naval Observatory, in 1867, gives it as his deliberate judgment, that in the previous history of that observatory, three-fifths of its record is practically blank, and that the astronomical output of the remaining two-fifths is quite as good as could have been expected with unsuitable instruments and untrained observers.

The new Transit Circle set up in 1865, with which to make observations for what has been declared the principal object of the Naval Observatory, has proved a source of endless perplexity to the observers, and a fruitful theme for the scoffs and gibes of astronomers who are well versed in this class of work. It is quite possible that these observations are no worse than those which have been made at some other observatories; but they are certainly inferior to those made at Green-wich, Cape of Good Hope, Paris, Berlin and Leyden, and very decidedly inferior to those made at Pulkowa. A part of this apparent inferiority may really be due to errors of computation and printing which are excessively frequent in some of the annual volumes produced by the Observatory,—notably in that for 1868. If our Naval Observatory were a small, ill-nurtured institution ; if it had experienced niggardly instead of most generous treatment from the Government; if its superintendents had not repeatedly declared this work with the Transit Circle to be the most important work of the Observatory ; the results might be entitled to more lenient judgment.

Work With the Great Telescope.

In 1873, the great equatorial telescope, at that time the most power-ful in existence, was placed in position. It has been devoted chiefly to the observation of double stars and of the satellites (or moons) of the large planets. Determinations of the distances of the stars, studies upon nebulas and planets, and other minor observations, have also formed a part of the work done with this instrument. It was with this instrument that Professor Hall made his memorable discovery of the moons of Mars. The observations made with the great telescope are believed to be standard in precision. In special lines, such as the obser-vation of faint planetary satellites, they are scarcely surpassed else-where in amount and value. It is largely upon work done with this instrument that the Naval Observatory relies for whatever of reputation, as a place where observations are made, it enjoys. Yet this work is entirely outside of its principal official programme. When placed on its defense, the representatives of the observatory try to maintain that such work forms but an incidental and insignificant part of its activity.

To some extent this claim is justified. Usually two, and rarely more than three persons, as astronomers and computers, have been engaged in work with this instrument in any one year. At a high estimate these form not more than twenty per cent. of the effective working-staff at the observatory,—usually less. The great telescope has constituted an observatory within an observatory. The astronomer in charge has been virtually his own superintendent; and perhaps the superintendents of the observatory are entitled to some praise for permitting this to be so, under the circumstances.

At different periods, with intervals of comparative inaction, observa-tions of comets and small planets (sometimes of other objects) have been made with the smaller telescope. At one time, 1853-1861, this was about the only sign of astronomical activity that emanated from the Observatory. It is not known that these observations are entitled to consideration beyond that which attaches to good routine observations of the kind, constantly produced in many of the large and small observatories. Such work has a value. In order, however, to acquire for it more than an incidental and secondary value, it must be prosecuted continuously through long periods, on some consistent and comprehensive plan, that attends to distinct needs. There is no evidence that such a plan has governed this work at the Naval Observatory. Exceptional years excluded, the observations are not numerous enough to call for special remark.

Meteorology, Magnetism and Miscellaneous.

So far as meteorological observations are concerned, those of the Naval Observatory have been of a simple routine character, but they have been made with diligence and regularity by the watchmen under direction of one of the astronomers. The "night watching in stormy weather" has, after all, fallen to the lot of civilians, who have not even had the stimulus of a military "duty to compel a flagging inclination."

After marked inattention to the subject of terrestrial magnetism, supposed by the founders of the observatory to be peculiarly worthy the notice of a naval institution, the Observatory, in 1887, finally inaugurated a magnetical department, the buildings for which were provided by the Hydrographic office. This subject has apparently interested the younger officers stationed at the Observatory. But already in his report for 1890, we find the Superintendent saying that the "services of a laborer" at a salary of $720 per annum "are urgently required." This "laborer," in addition to the care of the little buildings, or rooms (which would doubtless prove too much of a burden to the seven laborers already employed, as well as to the two "skilled laborers"), could "read and record temperatures," "develop photographs, make prints and do other work, which at present takes up much of the time of the officers in charge that could be more profitably employed." It is the old story. The details of scientific work are as irksome to military men, as the routine duties of the military camp or vessel of war would be to scientific men.

The Naval Observatory rates chronometers for the Navy. This work has been done by naval officers in recent years; and in connection with it an elaborate public time service has been maintained, resulting in considerable friction with private observatories. This department has doubtless been maintained in a sufficiently creditable manner. This is the work of a Naval Observatory.

Astronomical Researches by the Professors.

Since 1861, there has emanated from the Naval Observatory a series of astronomical memoirs, usually in the form of "Appendices" to the annual volume. Some of these have earned a deservedly high reputation, and are not surpassed in value by the similar contributions from any other observatory in the world. Many of these researches have been published elsewhere than in the Observatory volumes. For whatever of reputation among astronomers that it enjoys, the Naval Observatory is more indebted to these memoirs than to its work in observation. In 1877, the Superintendent, in an attempt to defend the existing organization of the observatory, cited some facts to show the appreciation in which it was held abroad. (Report of the Secretary of the Navy for 1877, pp. 317-9). Among other things the space devoted to the Naval Observatory in the "German Astronomical Review" was counted up. This was really no test of the value of observatory work, or a very imperfect one at least. It was shown that this space amounted to 104½ pages. But of these 104½ pages, 59 pages, or more than half, were devoted to the personal researches of Professor Newcomb; so that if this is a test of appreciation for observatory work considerably more than half of it in this case is due to the volunteer efforts of one man out of the fifteen or twenty employed. One is tempted to speculate as to what might have been the result if Professor Newcomb had been given the power to direct the labors of the others as efficiently as he did his own.

In fact, very little of favorable comment upon the work of the Naval Observatory will be anywhere found that does not relate to such of the "Appendices" as contain the personal researches of the Professors of Mathematics, without special connection with the observations of the Observatory. The work with the Transit Circle, Yarnall's Catalogue, and other purely observational work of the observatory have been the subjects of occasional descriptive comment.

Those of the "Appendices" which contain general memoirs upon subjects of astronomical research not specially founded upon observations made at the Naval Observatory, with the briefer contributions to astronomical journals upon theoretical subjects, while they are the most creditable part of its record, have little or nothing to do with its principal function as an institution where observations are made. They were almost invariably volunteer works, undertaken solely at the instance of the authors themselves, who were not in any sense directed to perform them. There was never a superintendent at the Naval Observatory who could have presumed to exercise any actual supervision over these works, further than to permit them to be done, and to say how much time and money could be spared for the purpose, in addition to extra-official work. The superintendents are, of course, entitled to whatever of praise is due to them for aiding these works in some cases, and for permitting them to be done.

Respects in which the Naval Observatory has Failed.

It is quite evident from the record, that the Naval Observatory has not achieved the place in the annals of astronomy which might have been expected from the generous support which it has received. For the first seventeen years it was astronomically a failure. .This judgment is very well and fairly expressed in the comments of Professor Newcomb, previously quoted. The period from 1861 to about 1868 was one of development. During this time the Observatory was successively in charge of the two superintendents who, alone, out of the entire list, could lay even a moderate claim to professional standing in astronomy. Later, the record of the Observatory has been uneven and, on the whole, distinctly unsatisfactory; and during the last six or eight years it has degenerated into a lifeless and unproductive routine.

The chief trouble has often been pointed out by astronomers. There has been no evidence that the activities of the Observatory are based on any specific and controlling plan. Its work, like that of many small observatories, has been desultory and without cumulative effect. This is made more plain and definite in this way. Each of the great national observatories has striven to become authority in some important field of work. Greenwich leads in the thoroughness, abundance, and continuity of its observations upon the principal stars and the bodies of the solar system. Pulkowa is foremost in observations of fundamental precision upon the stars visible to unassisted vision, and in the determination of astronomical constants pertaining to that class of observations. The Paris National Observatory has gained leadership in photography of precision upon the stars. The Cape of Good Hope Observatory occupies for the Southern hemisphere the field corresponding to that held by Greenwich in the Northern; and, besides, is foremost in micrometric work with the heliometer. The Berlin Observatory, with its related Computing bureau, has become authority in regard to the small planets; and Potsdam Observatory is the leader in the more recondite researches by the spectroscope and photography, where these depend on accurate measurements. Bonn has been foremost in the uranometry of the northern sky, Cordoba in that of the southern; each in its sphere having also led in the comprehensive observation of telescopic stars. The list might be prolonged, but these illustrations will suffice to show that while each of these observatories has made valuable contributions in varied lines of research, they are each of them *authority* in some one or more related lines. For instance, any one desiring immediate information, without absolute completeness, in these respective lines, would naturally consult the work of these observatories first; and they would be apt to test the value of similar observations elsewhere, by inquiring whether it comes up to the standard of these observatories. It would be natural to say in praise of the work of a given observatory, that it was nearly or quite as good as the similar work of one of these observatories in that line. That would be considered praise sufficient to settle the matter. The Naval Observatory has made the best and most numerous observations upon the fainter moons of the planets. Otherwise, there is scarcely a point in which that observatory would be considered by astronomers to have made a distinctly leading record. Otherwise no observatory would feel complimented by having it said that its observations in a particular line are as good as the corresponding observations of Washington. Outside the work done by means of the great Equatorial, since 1873, the absolute destruction of all the observations ever made at the Naval Observatory would not sensibly delay the progress of research in any line. The point in this statement is not that the work is not fairly good, but that none of it is so good and unique as to be indispensable—not so good but that equally good or better, covering the same ground, cannot be found elsewhere. The Naval Observatory has not been a leader.

Nevertheless, ever since the administration of Captain Gilliss, the Observatory has had a large corps of able assistants. It is not assuming too much to say that it is not inferior to the astronomical staff of any other observatory. But as a rule there has been an apparent lack of zeal in the observations, where in the stress of scientific competition, zeal is so necessary. The causes of this cannot readily be stated with precision. They may originate in a variety of sources to be considered later on. Badly planned instruments would be one cause. Another would be the feeling that, owing to the absence of a well-defined aim and an equally defined plan, the results could not rise above commonplace in usefulness. They would be merely imitative, and would have no distinctive value. They would not be likely to be hereafter cited to determine any particular thing which could not be as well or better determined through other evidence. The observations savor too much of unthinking and unprofitable routine. The professors, therefore, would feel like saving their energies for their own personal researches, rather than to spend them in wheeling the sands of the seashore with aimless industry from one point to another. The lack of comprehensive schemes of investigation in which the labors of many can be coördinated, so as to produce an impressive whole, as at Pulkowa, is also responsible to some extent for the present state of things. In short, the Observatory has been without a directing head. The superintendents, wisely recognizing their inability to direct the scientific labors, in the manner suggested, have had the tact and discretion to perceive that the best thing under the circumstances, would be to leave the chief assistants to do as they please. It was probably the wisest course; but no great observatory can ever be built up in that way. Millions spent on marble palaces and costly apparatus, would serve only to emphasize the failure.

Opinion of the Superintendent of the Naval Observatory.

These views upon the recent history of the Observatory may appear hypercritical. There is no institution of the kind in which one may not easily pick flaws. It is much easier to criticise astronomical observations, than it is to make good ones. It will, therefore be interesting to call in the judgment of the Superintendent of the Naval Observatory in the case.

Consider, then, the progress of annual expenditure for current maintenance of the Observatory. This may begin with 1867, when the Observatory was relieved of the care of the charts. Exclude extraordinary expenditures, amounting to $570,000. (See appended Note B.) The figures for all purposes cannot be very exactly given without recourse to the records on file in the appropriate departments. But it is possible to form fair estimates. From such estimates it will appear that the total resources of the Naval Observatory have amounted to an annual average, in the period, 1867 to 1873, of $47,000; from 1873 to 1879, of $56,000; from 1879 to 1885, of $60,500; and from 1885 to 1891 of $60,800. (Appended Note B.) It may be thought that the salaries of line officers of the Navy ought not to be included in these estimates, on the ground that the same number would have to be maintained whether they were assigned to the Observatory or not. In that case, the annual averages would be : for the period, 1867 to 1873, about $36,580; for 1873 to 1879, about $43,170 ; for 1879 to 1885, about $41,040 ; and for 1885 to 1891, about $43,340. (Appended Note B.) On either hypothesis, there has evidently been no material diminution in the total resources of the Naval Observatory during the six years, 1885 to 1891, as compared with the six years of the period, 1873 to 1879.

It might be inferred, therefore, that the efficiency of the Observatory has been well maintained of late, especially as the average resources from 1889 to 1891 (for the two fiscal years) were perceptibly larger than for the other years with which they are grouped. No great surprise ought to be felt, if it should turn out that added experience of the astronomical corps, inspired by the increasing development of astronomy, had quickened the pulses of the observatory in a sensible degree. On this point, the present Superintendent, in his annual report for the year ending June 30, 1890, says :

"The issuing of the annual volumes of the observatory has been for years falling farther and farther behind, until now publication is five years behind the observations, and the amount of work done has been growing less and less. Important improvements in instruments and in methods of observation, as well as new and equally important lines of research, many of which are actively pushed forward at the principal Government observatories, have here been entirely neglected on account of the lack of practical astronomers to make independent observations and to carry on special investigations in conjunction with other observatories. In this connection, it is much to be regretted that from the cause just mentioned this observatory was unable to perform its part in observing the positions of the stars in the zone assigned to complete a chart of the heavens." (Report of the Secretary of the Navy for 1890, p. 99.)

It is proper to add that the Superintendent prefaces the above extract from his report with the following statement :

"Out of the corps of twelve professors of mathematics in the Navy, there are now only six who are on duty as astronomers; one of the ablest of these will be retired shortly, leaving but five for service at the Observatory and Nautical Almanac office. In contrast with this there were in 1876, and for several years about that time, six professors of mathematics, well known as astronomers, engaged in active work at the observatory alone."

The number of professors under the orders of the superintendent from 1885 to the present time has been five,—all astronomers; and three of them are among the number alluded to by the Superintendent as well known astronomers in 1876, the others coming in under the system of rigid examinations in vogue for appointments to that corps. The effective reduction in the number of professors has not, therefore, been very great ; and it should have been compensated in some measure by the increase of four or five in the number of naval officers on duty at the Observatory in the latter period.

Astronomers, the world over, who have given much attention to the matter, will cordially agree with the present Superintendent in his main conclusions. But they do not agree with the idea of the Superintendent that this unfortunate state of affairs is altogether due to "the lack of practical astronomers to make independent observations." When that opinion was written there were on duty at the observatory, exclusive of naval officers, at least eight men, who are entitled to be called practical observers and astronomers. Few observatories in the world can show a list larger than this. Rarely has so large an annual appropriation for general and contingent expenses been available for the use of any government observatory. In the sum total, the resources for an observatory of the first rank have always been provided in undiminishing amount. If these are not so applied as to maintain the full efficiency of the institution, there must be something wrong with the system.

SECTION VI.— NAVAL OFFICERS AS ASTRONOMERS.

One of the reasons why the scientific prosperity of the Observatory appears to bear no definite relation to its total resources in men and money at any time, can be attributed to the fact that naval officers are not necessarily, in virtue of their commissions, trained astronomers, or scientific men. This statement implies no disrespect to naval officers,— any more than the assertion that our great statesmen are not, as a rule, skilled musicians could be regarded as derogatory to them. The people, recalling the facts of a glorious history, feel the greatest confidence in our naval officers in their professional capacity. Our naval officers have shown themselves to be skillful and diligent in matters concerning their own profession; courteous and manly representatives of their country in times of peace; cool and reasonable in irritating relations; energetic and decisive in emergencies; chivalrous and intrepid in fight. But all this public esteem and admiration, which they have justly earned and now deserve, does not entitle them to preside over our courts of justice, to manage our hospitals, or to superintend our observatories.

Why, then, do we find our Government observatory in the hands of naval officers?

One motive for placing the Observatory in the hands of the Navy, had its origin in the excess of naval officers, and in the belief that this excess could be profitably employed in astronomy. This excess was very great at the time the Observatory was founded. (See Report of the Secretary of the Navy, for 1845.) It was so great that, in the words of Secretary Bancroft, some of them "since their promotions have not received orders, and, from the excess of officers and for other reasons, can never receive them." At the same time our vessels of war could not sail up the Potomac to the capital of the nation without charts procured from the Admiralty office in England. (Report of Lieutenant Maury, for 1845). The Government of that day appears to have preferred to employ our naval officers in astronomy, rather than in maritime surveying; though it may be doubted if this preference extended to the officers themselves. That the Observatory did afford a refuge for a goodly part of this excess of naval officers is well known. For instance, in the introduction of the Observatory volume for 1851-2, it is stated that forty-five officers were on duty there during those two years, the term of service averaging about eight months for each. The astronomical observations for those years are conceded to be practically worthless.

The attempt to convert naval officers into astronomers has never succeeded and cannot succeed unless the officer, as in the case of Captain Gilliss, virtually abandons his profession. The young man who joins the Navy because he has a strong taste for it is not likely to have the temperament necessary to make a successful scientific investigator. The astronomical observations made by line officers of the Navy at the observatory are relatively few and inferior. This can be specifically shown with reference to the observations they have made with the meridian instruments upon the sun, moon, planets, and telescopic stars. The observations they made with the " prime vertical transit " in 1845 have been shown by Professor Hall to have for each observation only one-third the value of those made with the same instrument by experienced astronomers in 1862 to 1867. (Astronomical Journal, Vol. X., p. 57.)

After an interval of nearly thirty years in which no astronomical observations of scientific consequence had been attempted by officers of the naval line, a systematic and persistent effort was made in the period, 1882 to 1885, to employ these officers in astronomical observations. This aroused protests in the public press, but the officers persevered.* Except for the injury they might do the scientific reputation of the country, and for the diversion of their energies into a channel having nothing in common with the purpose for which they were educated at the expense of the Government, there was, perhaps, no valid reason why they should not make the experiment. The Government can have the services of any number of astronomers likely to be required, at rates of compensation no greater than the naval officers receive, without incurring one dollar of expenditure, either in the preliminary or in the professional education of these persons.

The observations which one of the senior officers made upon comets and small planets, with the smaller equatorial telescope, were numerous and have been published. It is probable that they are of fair quality. Such observations are of the class which the beginner finds it easiest to master. They had not the remotest connection with any nautical or naval utility.

Other officers observed the sun, moon and planets with the transit instrument. These observations are also published. They are

---

* An anonymous writer, " N," evidently representing the naval line at the observatory, wrote a communication to the New York Tribune, defending the policy of the Superintendent in this controversy. This article, which appears in the issue of the Tribune for Feb. 12, 1883, maintains among other points strongly put :

" 4. The officers engaged upon this work were selected for their mathematical and scientific attainments, and in the former at least will stand comparison with a majority of the professors of mathematics."

' Again, he says : " The Naval Observatory is supported at government expense for naval purposes and while in addition to its special uses other scientific work may be done, it has never been the policy of this country to sustain establishments for purely scientific investigations. The most important duty at the Naval Observatory is the testing, rating and care of the chronometers, collecting data for the Nautical Almanac, and sending time signals and dropping time balls at the various stations. These are purely naval wants which can be readily supplied by naval officers."

These extracts, in connection with arguments used in the official reports, which are of an altogether different tenor, well illustrate the cleverness of some of those who favor naval control of the observatory in misleading public sentiment. To the public they say, this is purely a practical Naval Observatory. But they well know that if they should say this officially in a way to attract the notice of astronomers, they could be at once convicted of the most outrageous extravagance. If that position is true the naval officers have absolutely squandered nearly $40,000 per annum in useless expenditure for the observatory, and $600,000 in expenditures for the new observatory. The public is told that naval officers are competent astronomers. It is possible that public officers and Congressmen, in private conversations, are led to suppose that every naval officer is necessarily an astronomer. But no such claim would be made in the presence of professional astronomers. Whenever added support for the observatory is needed, the request is put upon the ground that the observatory is a great scientific institution, and it is said : * * * " It is necessary to appoint some professors of mathematics, astronomers of known experience, as it is mainly to this corps that the observatory has to look for aid to keep up its astronomical reputation." (Rep. of the Secretary of the Navy for 1890, p. 99.) The arguments for removal of the observatory to the new site, with the attendant enormous expenditure, were exclusively based upon the necessity of maintaining and increasing the scientific glories of the establishment. On any other ground the proposal would have been simply impudent. The authorities should insist upon knowing definitely, once for all, what kind of an observatory the Naval Observatory officially claims to be. The law does not say.

decidedly inferior to the observations made by civilian astronomers at the same time in the opposite wing of the observatory building, though the latter were obliged to include an operation which doubled the difficulty of the observation, and which the instrument used by the naval officers did not permit to be employed. Mathematically weighed, one observation of the sun by the trained astronomers is worth about as much as three by the naval officers. In the matter of general reliability, the contrast would be, without doubt, more unfavorable to the work of the naval officers.

Still other officers observed with the prime vertical transit. These observations have never been published, and nothing is known to the astronomical public as to their number or quality.

Occasionally, junior officers have served as routine computers, though the amount of such work done by them is not relatively important. If they are patient under such tasks, there is no reason why, after a few months of training, they should not render efficient service. Such service some of them have produced, as evidenced by the testimony of astronomers for whom it was rendered. Indeed, one may cheerfully concede that the naval officers are men of much more than average intelligence. The manner of their original appointment secures this. But it by no means follows that they can become skilled astronomers for independent work in the intervals of their regular professional duties.

This appears to have been the conclusion of the late Admiral John Rodgers, a former superintendent of the observatory. He says:

"No corps in which observatory work is casual, to be abandoned upon occasion for the proper duties of another profession, can compete with the observatories of Europe, in which astronomical observations are a life-long pursuit." (Report of the Secretary of the Navy for 1877, p. 320.)

On July 1, 1886, these observations by officers of the naval line appear to have been definitely abandoned, and it is not likely that the experiment will soon be resumed. Neither Congress nor the Navy department could make astronomers from naval officers, but through an arrangement by which astronomers are sometimes appointed to be "Professors of Mathematics in the United States Navy," it has become possible to claim that the Observatory is really a naval establishment which employs chiefly "officers of the Navy."

The pursuit of astronomical investigation, like that of all the other exact sciences, is a profession, requiring for its ordinary walks fully as much preliminary training as is required for the successful practice of law or medicine, and for its higher departments, in their way, as much natural aptitude, training and experience, as are necessary to the development of the qualities of statesmanship in the legal practitioner, or of the power to make independent discoveries in the healing art by the physician. Mathematical and astronomical training at the Naval

Academy is certainly not superior to that which is furnished at our leading colleges and technical schools, and very probably inferior to that which is afforded to students of optional courses in these institutions. Yet the students of our colleges and universities when they first enter the astronomical observatories are considered to be, and are actually found to be, mere beginners in the science of astronomy. They have at best some elementary notions of the science, and if previously trained in the proper way, are ready to make a good beginning,—but nothing more. They are still in need of professional training.

Lieutenant Gilliss, who was well aware of what was needed, proposed to give the midshipmen such training at the observatory. He says:

"They should possess a knowledge of the higher mathematics, and a taste for astronomical pursuits. To such requisites they must add patience, perseverance, and endurance; for the refinements of astronomy entail long hours of delicate adjustments and calculations, as well as continued loss of sleep, and exposure to the external temperature at all seasons. Such officers it may be somewhat difficult to select immediately; but, with an eye to the future, inducements should be offered midshipmen to give greater attention to study. Mathematics being the groundwork, upon which must be built all scientific knowledge, I recommend to serious consideration the propriety of offering to the five midshipmen who annually pass the best examination in its higher branches, the *honor* of serving four years at the observatory. If no others are ordered, I think the emulation will be such in a few years that the junior officers will deservedly attain a high character among scientific men." (Pp. 66 and 67, Senate Doc., No. 114, 28th Cong., 2d session. Feb. 7, 1845.)

This proposal was not adopted, and evidently could not be consistently adopted so long as the Government is always able to command the services of trained astronomers without offering a bounty, and without incurring the smallest expense for their education. Yet it was the only method by which astronomers could be developed from the Navy, or from any other walk in life.

What actually took place is learned from the comments of Lieutenant Maury, Superintendent, as well as from other sources. He says:

"A large corps, principally consisting of lieutenants and passed midshipmen is engaged upon the details of these investigations [wind and current charts]. They are liable to be called away to sea, and often are at a moment's warning; and that so frequently, that almost the entire corps is sometimes ordered off to sea and a new one sent in its place, so as to form, in the course of a few weeks, a complete change of the officers engaged upon these investigations." (Washington Observations for 1846; published, 1851.)

Even when applied to the simple clerical details required of assistants on those wind and current investigations, the system proved vexatious, and called forth complaint from the very man who, as much as any one, was responsible for it. The term of shore duty at present appears to be more regular than it formerly was; but even with three years of it, the young officer must go to sea just at the time when he could begin to be useful in the scientific operations.

It is indeed true that very many of our American astronomers are practically self-taught. With time and opportunity, the resolute man, filled with enthusiasm for his chosen science can conquer all obstacles. But it requires both time and opportunity, and these struggles cannot be commingled with the distractions of another profession.

SECTION VII.— REASONS WHY ASTRONOMICAL WORK SHOULD BE DIRECTED BY AN ASTRONOMER, AND CAUSES OF THE FAILURE OF THE SUPERINTENDENTS OF THE NAVAL OBSERVATORY.

But if it is difficult for the naval officer to acquire the rudiments of the astronomical profession, how much more hopeless must it seem for him to accumulate that ripened experience, those broad views of astronomy, and that keen discernment of the present tendencies of investigation, so necessary in the man who is to supervise, direct, and inspire the labors of others in an institution mainly devoted to professional research in astronomy.

The acknowledged scientific inefficiency of the Naval Observatory is very largely due to the lack of skilled superintendence. A man who should boast that he never saw a ship or a cannon, and that none of his subordinates ever had, would never be entrusted with the command of a ship or squadron about to engage the enemy. Yet the first Superintendent of the observatory made much of the fact that he had never seen an astronomical "instrument of the kind before and had no one with [him] who had." It is not surprising that the Naval Observatory under such captaincy has been beaten.

The Superintendent Must Choose a Field of Work.

In the first place, the superintendent of any observatory must determine what is the best and most appropriate field of work for it. This cannot be left in a hap-hazard way to the tastes of the subordinate astronomers. Nor is it any longer justifiable to devote the energies of a great observatory to those researches alone, which tend to the "improvement of the art of navigation," even in the most sublimated theoretical sense. That department of astronomy must be looked after, to supply its real needs, in precisely the same way that obtains with other branches of the science. The field of astronomical research is widening as it never has before since the days of Newton and his successors. All the great astronomical centers feel the force of this. The Greenwich Observatory has made provision for a large telescope (diameter of glass, 28 inches) with a view to attacking some of these new problems with greater effect. It has already set up a new photographic telescope, and is pursuing with great energy the preliminary investigations in celestial photography of precision, so necessary for its own guidance and for that of others. The Greenwich Observatory which, for one hundred and forty years, has accomplished far more than any other in furnishing the material of observation for the improvement of planetary theories and for "finding the so much desired longitude at sea," while it will continue to give more attention to that department of astronomy than any other observatory can afford to give, will hereafter expend the greater part of its energies in other fields. The Royal Observatory at the Cape, belongs to the best type of modern development. Its field of work has been completely transformed. Pulkowa is already, and has been since its foundation, engaged in a line, the relative importance of which must steadily increase with time. Within the past two decades it has also added a department of astro-physics. The observational energies of the Paris National Observatory are stirred to a degree which that institution has not heretofore known. For many years the numerous German observatories under government patronage have been employed in investigations, preparing the way to the modern revival, both of mathematical and physical astronomy.

Each of these institutions is finding its own work. It will not do for a great observatory to content itself with merely imitating them, and performing the coöperative tasks suggested by them. Neither should a particular task be avoided because it has been elsewhere undertaken. The highest technical experience is needed in order to decide wisely in this choice of work. The business of a national observatory lies in the lines of established promise, and not in those of mere speculation or experimentation. Observations necessary to supply the needs of the public service must, of course, be attended to by the national observatory, but these will never require a large force of observers or expensive equipment.

In this choice of work, the superintendent has no safe guide, otherwise than in his own knowledge of astronomical needs, founded upon an intimate acquaintance with the history of modern astronomy, and of its tendencies up to the present. He must know not only what it is practicable to do, and what needs to be done, but also what is likely to prove the most profitable investment of future labor. He must look ahead and see, as well as he can, what is coming. His assistants cannot do this for him. They can advise, but the decision rests with him. They may be able to choose some special line of work and gain leadership in it, but they can rarely extend this to a whole department, provide for the employment of their colleagues, and insure uninterrupted continuance of the work.

Choice of the works most appropriate for an observatory would be easier were it not for the constantly changing aspect of astronomical development. This feature of change is more marked at the present time than it has ever been during the last two centuries. The astronomy of twenty years ago is now termed "old-fashioned," that of twenty years hence will have a similar epithet for us. While many overestimate the influence and importance of this crowding novelty in the methods and substance of research, there is no doubt that it must be intelligently and closely studied by all who have the responsibility of organizing astronomical work on a large scale. The question, how far not to yield, may be as important and difficult to decide as the opposite. If the superintendent does not successfully meet and decide these questions, the institution under his charge will get behind the times, just as the present Superintendent of the Naval Observatory says that institution now is.

The choice of work must be governed, to a great extent, by the special training and capacities of available assistants. Furthermore, it is important that assistants be directed, or guided, toward those spheres of activity for which they are respectively best fitted. Scientific discernment of a high order is required for the proper performance of this duty. The Naval Observatory has suffered from a defect in this respect.

The Direct Supervision of Work.

In an observatory so generously supported as the Naval Observatory has been, it may be possible to employ high-salaried assistants of eminent abilities and experience, who do not need constant supervision in the details of work. They should be permitted as much freedom in following their individual tastes as is compatible with the interests of the observatory as a whole ; but since the observatory is supported in response to a public demand, and not for the pleasure of individual men employed in its duties, there should be some one who possesses scientific ability and knowledge enough to devise a proper coördination of these individual tastes with the obligation of the observatory to the public, the interests of which it is the special business of the superintendent to ascertain and enforce. This is one of his most delicate, technically difficult and responsible duties, and it is one which the superintendent, who is not an astronomer, must entirely abdicate. So far as tact in dealing with men is concerned, it may be admitted that no astronomer could be expected to surpass the distinguished men who have hitherto filled the office of Superintendent of the Observatory, and if that were the only qualification required, there would be no occasion for change.

Also, when the director is an astronomer, a large proportion even of the important work of a great observatory can be performed by assistants who might not, perhaps, be able to do so well without professional guidance. It is so in all professions. It is necessary for the director in such case to see that assistants are competent to carry out his instructions, more or less detailed as may be required, and that they are faithful in the performance of duties assigned to them. The assistants must be not only physically present at times when duty requires such presence; they must not only manifest the outward form of industry, but they must be really accomplishing something useful. The two former requirements are probably as well looked after now at the Naval Observatory as they are in any other, but the latter requires personal inspection of the work while it is in progress by some one who knows how it ought to be done, and an examination of results, when furnished, by a director professionally competent to do this expeditiously and on his own independent judgment.

In this same connection it is proper to remark that it is an important responsibility of a superintendent to keep a watchful eye on the incidental needs of astronomy. He must suggest and plan the numerous small series of observations and minor researches, so necessary to the vigorous life as well as to the reputation of a large observatory. It is in these that the junior assistants find their opportunity to develop the power of independent research. It is a judicious admixture of this sort of work with the heavier operations of prolonged investigation that inspires the working staff with fresh zeal which extends its influence far beyond the official working hours of the establishment. The director, or superintendent, who by reason of his professional qualities is able to inspire his assistants with this zeal for scientific work, and who by reason of his experience and attainments is able to put his assistants fairly on the road to successful results, will never have to complain of unwilling service or inferior work. If he has not these qualities and this experience, then, perhaps, as Mr. Mallory said, military methods may be necessary "to compel a flagging inclination."

In all these respects the system of non-professional superintendence in vogue at the Naval Observatory has retarded its usefulness in a sensible degree. There have been periods when the Observatory seemed to be full of life and scientific interest; but analysis will show that it was a state brought about by the activity of two or three of the leading assistants, and that it did not have the element of permanence, because it did not spring from a source which acted equally upon the entire staff. The superintendent was not the scientific leader of the Observatory.

The Responsibility of Providing Instrumental Equipment.

To see that an observatory is provided with the best practicable equipment and observing arrangements, at the least possible cost, is another highly important duty of the astronomical director.

The equipment of the observatory at Pulkowa, as well as that for the Bonn Observatory was provided shortly before that for the Naval Observatory; and the meridian instruments then installed at the two former observatories for observations upon the stars and bodies of the solar system are still in efficient use and have not been supplemented by others during the fifty years that have passed. They are scarcely to be surpassed by the meridian instruments of the present day, if an opinion may be founded upon the work done with them. In the same period, Bessel, the greatest practical astronomer of the century, provided a new meridian instrument for the Prussian Observatory at Königsberg. Instruments of a similar construction, known as Transit Circles, had been in general use since the beginning of the century. These are the most important instrumental factor in assembling "data for computing a Nautical Almanac." Lieutenant Gilliss visited many observatories in Europe for the special purpose of obtaining advice as to the new equipment for the Naval Observatory. At that time he was a mere tyro in the art of astronomical observation; but very likely no astronomer in America at that time would have done better. This does not, however, impair the force of the illustration,—America was in that respect unfortunate. He was not able to weigh the conflicting advice he received, so as to arrive at a proper conclusion. He decided for the antiquated "Mural Circle." The consequence was that the Observatory was handicapped in its principal astronomical undertaking during the first twenty years of its existence; while brilliant results were being achieved through the use of the instruments procured, as stated, for the observatories at Pulkowa, Bonn, Königsberg, and elsewhere.

Soon after entering upon the duties of his position, the Superintendent of the Naval Observatory conceived the idea of a new instrument which he christened a "Refraction Circle." This was to perfect the means for gathering original material for the calculation of an American Almanac, as one may learn from his glowing descriptions which were published. The instrument was procured at great cost—a cost undoubtedly sufficient to have purchased a first-class Transit Circle. There is no record of any observations made with it. The tradition is that it "would not stand alone."

Even so late as 1865, when the new Transit Circle was procured to supersede the old meridian instruments, misfortune appears to have pursued the Observatory. One would have supposed that extraordinary care would have been exercised in the plan of an instrument which was to subserve the principal object of the Observatory and employ one-third, or more, of its effective astronomical staff. Yet it has been regarded by astronomers generally as a failure. If it be maintained that the inferior results obtained through its use are to be attributed to incompetent observers, or to incompetent direction, rather than to defects of the instrument, how shall the fact be explained that this instrument is now undergoing reconstruction at an expense nearly sufficient to buy a new instrument?

It was at first supposed that better observations could be made with this instrument in a new room, since that in which it was first placed was unquestionably not well suited to the purpose. The official record tells the story of the success experienced in this new enterprise, which, by the way, did not do away with the particular defects of the observations that were most injurious.

Report of Commodore B. F. Sands, Superintendent, Sept. 25, 1869.

"The architectural qualities of the new room have not yet been tested, but there is no doubt that for purely astronomical purposes it is the best meridian observing room in the world."

Report of Rear Admiral B. F. Sands, Superintendent, Oct. 6, 1871.

"The new wing built for it [Transit Circle] has answered our expectations, but will yet require some fitting up, for which I have submitted an estimate."

Report of Rear Admiral C. H. Davis, Superintendent, Oct. 17, 1874.

"The Transit Circle observing-room is in a very unsatisfactory condition. It is impossible to obtain proper ventilation in the hot days of midsummer; the roof-shutters do not work well; and, in spite of frequent repairs, they leak in every heavy rain-storm ; the track for the reversing-carriage, is not properly laid ; the arms of the reversing-carriage, which are half an inch too near together, require some changes ; and the protection of the thermometer, on which the computation for refraction depends, is such that there is frequently an abnormal range of 5° or 6°."
"It will require at least $1,500 to put this room in order."

In 1874, a splendid new telescope, then the most powerful in existence, was mounted at the Naval Observatory. It cost, with building and fittings, $67,000. The observational record with this instrument has been highly creditable. The work, however, is entirely in the field of pure scientific investigation. Yet the authorities of the Observatory appear to have decided that this instrument must be almost totally reconstructed at the enormous expense of $32,600. The removal of this telescope to the new site and placing it in position, with incidental improvements that may really be necessary would cost a large sum to be sure ; but it requires a generous Government to pass over in silence this much greater expenditure upon an instrument which is still virtually new, and with the aid of which so much excellent work has been already accomplished.

This entire record in regard to instrumental equipment is in striking contrast to that of all other observatories, where the instruments have been provided under the direction of competent astronomers. The number of serious mistakes which have been made by them in this matter is surprisingly small.

Scientific Atmosphere of a Large Observatory.

Another important obligation of an astronomical superintendent is to see that his assistants are properly instructed in their duties. Even after his three or four years of apprenticeship the young observer has still much to learn at the hands of experience. He may gain this knowledge through the mistakes he will inevitably make. The liability to make such mistakes of method, and to waste labor upon comparatively profitless objects, is a serious drawback for the small observatories which cannot always command the services of an experienced astronomer. To a cértain extent no instruction can entirely do away with these errors of practice. But it is the duty of the director to be alert to discover these faults, or to see that they are pointed out, and, so far as possible, to correct them before they have resulted in the disfigurement of what might otherwise become creditable work. A great observatory can command the services of a director competent to perform this service ; if it neglects this opportunity, it sacrifices its advantage, and becomes wasteful of labor.

In short, it devolves upon the superintendent, vastly more than upon any of his subordinates, to create a healthy and vigorous scientific atmosphere in the observatory ; to stimulate study for the enthusiasm which it generates ; to nurture an *esprit de corps;* and to create a sentiment in the entire staff that will not tolerate the production of an inferior article of observation or research.

Editorial Duties of the Superintendent.

An intimate knowledge of the professional literature of astronomy is of essential use when the director is dealing with observations and deductions drawn from them. The practical questions come up : Shall they be accepted for printing in the form and condition presented ? How do they compare in method and value with similar observations and researches elsewhere produced ? Are they accurate in the details of observation and calculation ? It is easy to say off-hand, " we have beaten Greenwich all hollow " (Maury to Blackford, p. 49, Life of Maury), but it is quite another thing to determine the value of astronomical work by a specific examination. While it may not be necessary for the superintendent always to enter into every detail of such an examination, the experienced astronomer will know how to determine the general quality of the work in such a manner that he can afford to assume genuine responsibility for its character. The theory at the Naval Observatory appears to have been that these editorial functions could be, for the most part, omitted, and for the remainder, delegated to subordinates. Common sense and experience prove that subordinates hesitate to throw discredit on the work of a colleague, even when it is strongly justified. The exercise of such functions by those who do not have the real power of decision and who may be subjected to the vexatious duty of defending themselves against frivolous complaints of injustice, not only impairs the sense of actual responsibility, but is also a fruitful source of those jealousies which are complained of at the Naval Observatory.

Especially must the superintendent be responsible for the accuracy of the calculations and of printing. The directors of the great national observatories have always been very punctilious on these points. The annual volumes of the Naval Observatory bear ample testimony to the fact that this necessary function of the superintendent has not always been exercised with efficiency. A single example will suffice to illustrate. In 1873 the Observatory issued what is technically known as a star-catalogue. This is the only general catalogue containing the positions of a large number of stars which has so far emanated from the Observatory. It was hailed with joy by astronomers everywhere; for, although it had nothing whatever to do with the practice of navigation, it was the most important work of observation which had been published by the Observatory. But it was soon found to be crowded with errors to such an extent that a new edition was rendered imperatively necessary. This new and improved edition of " Yarnall's Catalogue " was issued in 1878. In the course of a very short time it was found that this new edition was still extremely faulty. The entire work was accordingly again revised, requiring years of skilled labor for the purpose. A third edition was finally brought out in 1890, which is presumably of the proper standard of accuracy. The catalogue must now be regarded as one of decided value.

This incident furnishes a most instructive illustration of the evils which may result from the lack of efficient superintendence. It is not alone the waste in costly printing, amounting to thousands of dollars, that calls for condemnation. It is the waste of labor in these repeated revisions, preparation of new manuscript, and extra proof-reading, that is equally to be deplored. The loss of prestige for the Observatory and for American astronomy, as well as the annoyances and waste of labor which astronomers have suffered in consequence of these faulty editions, cannot be ignored. This was the fault of unskilled superintendence.

Advantages of a Long Term of Service in the Superintendency of an Observatory.

Another obvious advantage of skilled civilian direction for an astronomical observatory is that resulting from the long tenure of office that becomes possible under that system. During fifty years the Pulkowa Observatory had two directors. Sir George B. Airy was in charge of the Greenwich Observatory for forty-five years; and during somewhat more than two centuries the directors of the Greenwich Observatory have numbered only eight. The Naval Observatory has had nine Superintendents during the past twenty-five years, and six of these since 1882. One advantage of the long term principle is the relatively small loss of efficiency, inevitable while a new superintendent is adjusting himself to his duties. A vastly greater advantage, however, lies in the possibility of originating and fixing those comprehensive and well-studied scientific policies which are so absolutely essential to the highest success in any scientific work, and especially in that of a great national observatory. The observatory thus becomes an astronomical power that makes an indelible impress upon the age. If the policy is ever a mistaken one, the astronomical superintendent will find it out more quickly and surely than any business man can.

Objections to Skilled Superintendence Considered.

Arguments have been presented on the other side of this question, between skilled and unskilled superintendence. Some of these have been met in the foregoing remarks. It is desirable, perhaps, that still others should receive attention.

" It is to be feared," says the late Admiral John Rodgers, Superintendent, " that a national observatory open to the whole body of American astronomers, would gravitate into the political arena, where mere unobtrusive merit would avail less than sectional partialities, or specious pleading supported by personal preferences." (Number 13 of papers accompanying the Report of the Secretary of the Navy for 1877.)

In this connection, it seems pertinent to inquire whether the Navy is more free from the operation of personal preferences and favoritism than are the civilian scientific bureaus of Government. It is confidently asserted that the civilian scientific bureaus have been remarkably free from partisan influences. With extremely rare exceptions, scientific men in positions of administrative responsibility, have sturdily defended the right and advisability of making appointments and promotions in scientific work under their charge, solely on the basis of personal and professional merit. That position has been almost invariably respected and supported by the higher executive powers. It is a notable fact of observation and remark, that the most intense partisans in Congress, and in positions of executive responsibility, have been among the most generous and intelligent of public men in regard to the non-partisan administration of scientific work. Scientific men seem to be regarded as non-combatants in the political arena, and are treated accordingly. The assertion may be safely ventured that the Coast Survey and Geological Bureau contain as large a proportion of " unobtrusive merit " among their employés, as the Naval Observatory contains, and that it would be as difficult to discover political motives in · the appointments to the former as. in the latter. There is no reason whatever for fearing that a different rule would prevail in regard to an astronomical observatory under civilian control.

The following extracts from the document prepared by the Superintendent of the Naval Observatory in 1877 (Report of the Secretary of the Navy, accompanying papers, No. 13) illustrate criticisms in reference to the superintendence of a large observatory by an astronomer, which have been brought forward in this controversy :

"The statement may, perhaps, be hazarded that authors, inventors, musicians, are naturally jealous of each others' professional reputation. It may be feared that mathematicians and astronomers are not free from the same weakness; and so far as this is true, so far would its existence militate against harmony and efficiency." (Admiral Rodgers.) * * * "No scientific man can afford to step from the ranks of scientific workers into such a position [as Superintendent of the observatory] unless he hopes to build up his reputation upon the labor of others." * * * "There are few eminent astronomers who have not made their reputation by the cultivation of some specialty to the exclusion of almost everything else; and were such a man made Superintendent of the observatory, there would be great danger that the whole force of the establishment would be employed in advancing his specialty; thus preventing his assistants from engaging in other work of equal or perhaps greater importance, and greatly limiting the scope of the institution." (Letter of majority professors to the Superintendent.)

It is fair to infer that Admiral Rodgers (who discusses the subject in a fair-minded way with predilections in favor of superintendence by an astronomer) had gained his experience in regard to the ways of scientific men at the Naval Observatory, of which he was then the honored Superintendent. It is pertinent to inquire whether there is anything in the system of administration at the Naval Observatory which should lead to the expression of opinions by astronomers*, so much at variance with those which are generally entertained in the profession elsewhere. It is quite as easy to suppose there was something of this kind as it is to believe that the members of a profession engaged in the noblest of intellectual pursuits are universally actuated by petty motives and selfish interests. It may be admitted that astronomers are no better in these respects than are lawyers, physicians, clergymen, or naval officers; but to say that they are not capable of self-government among themselves is to ignore the testimony of experience in the great as well as in the small national observatories of other lands. There is absolutely no escape from the logic of this experience except in saying that these charges apply to American astronomers only. One may admit, with the Superintendent, that troubles of an analogous nature are not unknown among professional musicians. Yet no one appears to have thought of a remedy like that which would be implied in placing a naval officer at the head of the Observatory. Whenever a great orchestra proves inharmonious in either sense of the word, the remedy which is always applied, whenever the public demand for music is strong enough to warrant it, is to put the refractory orchestra under the direction of the ablest musical director that available funds, or patronage, will warrant.

---

* Two of the Professors, Simon Newcomb, Superintendent of the Nautical Almanac, and Edward S. Holden, now director of the Lick Observatory in California, did not join in these views of their five colleagues, but wrote letters to the Superintendent, strongly advocating scientific control for the Observatory. It is also believed that the views of some of the other professors were subsequently very much modified.

It is further evident that the five majority professors did not want any superintendent at all, except a non-astronomical one who should, as they express it later in their letter, "look after the business affairs of the institution, thus leaving the scientific corps leisure for their proper work." This would undoubtedly, in some respects, prove an agreeable arrangement for those who suppose that a Government observatory exists, not in response to a public demand, but for the personal gratification of the astronomers who happen to be employed therein. The theory of a Government observatory has already been sufficiently considered. A national observatory exists, because the public at large desires that the nation shall bear its share in contributing to the intelligence of the world in a field which is one of the noblest and most fascinating that can engage the attention of mankind. At the same time this public relies on the assurance from astronomers that there is a large class of laborious operations in the most important fields of research which are very sure to be neglected, if left to the care of private enterprise. It is not for the assistants, nor even for the director, to dictate what work a national observatory shall do. The work is imposed upon the observatory by the logic of scientific events; and for that reason, especially, the director must be a well-trained and experienced astronomer, in order properly to perceive and interpret this logic. In nearly all countries having large observatories, he has a commission, or " board of visitors," to aid him in the performance of this duty, and to control him in this respect if his judgment be deemed at fault. In accepting the office and emoluments of a Government astronomer, whether subordinate or chief, the astronomer takes upon himself the obligation to labor faithfully in the interest of this public demand.

It is quite probable that an "eminent astronomer" would actually desire to make some distinct and possibly unique impression through the combined labors over which he might have the control. He would not wait for other observatories to point out the work he ought to do, nor fritter the energies confided to his management in doing the work which is as well, or better (and sufficiently), done elsewhere. Nor is there the least danger that an able specialist will dragoon unwilling assistants of high rank to labor in his own lines. He well knows that responsible work in science cannot be well done by the man who is not able to put some heart in it.

The majority professors, in common with other advocates of the present system of the Naval Observatory, make much of the business duties of the superintendent. They cannot be neglected ; but it is difficult to believe that they can be more onerous than the corresponding responsibilities of the Coast Survey or Geological Bureau. The superintendents of these establishments have been specially complimented by committees of Congress (Senate Reports, 49th Cong., 1st Session ; No. 1285, p. 52 ; and elsewhere) upon the ability and efficiency with which they have discharged this part of their duties; yet there has been no lack of attention to their scientific duties; and it is not known or believed that the chiefs of either of these important bureaus have at any time considered it necessary to recoup themselves for time spent in the multifarious business duties of their offices by stealing the credit due to their subordinates.

The Question of Comparative Expense.

Against proposed superintendence of our Government observatory by an astronomer has been urged the fear that the "expenses would be largely augmented." It is impossible to consider the matter of expenditure apart from that which is produced as the result of expenditure. Whether the expenses of the Observatory shall be increased or diminished under a civilian administration depends entirely upon the will of the people, expressed through their representatives in Congress, as to the amount and quality of astronomical product which is desirable that this nation shall contribute to the world's common stock of scientific, knowledge. The value of that product cannot be measured by the array of figures and the number of pages in publications. If it is considered sufficient that our Government observatory shall, hereafter, simply maintain its present scientific standing, and contribute astronomical results of not much more intrinsic value than those which have hitherto emanated from the Naval Observatory during like periods, then every experienced astronomer in the country (who is free to speak), would unite in the prediction that expenses would be reduced under the administration of a competent astronomer. The separation of the functions of the present establishment in such a manner, that the rating of the chronometers and similar duties shall be carried on at a naval observatory in charge of a naval officer, assisted by naval officers, and that the scientific duties, both theoretical and practical, shall be performed at an astronomical observatory in charge of a competent astronomer with a civilian organization, would unquestionably result in greater efficiency and economy of service.

In support of these assertions, two pertinent comparisons may be instituted. The Argentine National Observatory was established in 1872, ready for work. Its directors and assistants had been citizens of the United States, and received liberal salaries for their service. Every competent astronomer must join in the statement that the results achieved by the Argentine Observatory, at Cordoba, during the period from its foundation to 1885, were much greater in quantity and certainly not inferior in quality, as compared with the corresponding results produced by the United States Naval Observatory during any similar period of its history. Yet the annual expenditure at the Cordoba Observatory averaged less than $21,000, including sums expended for some buildings and instruments additional to those originally provided.

The current expenditures for the Naval Observatory, during this same period (1872–1885), exclusive of the salary of the superintendent and of line officers of the Navy, amounted to fully $42,000 *per annum*. (See Note B, appended.) The total expenditures for the Argentine Observatory were, in fact, less than the sums appropriated to the Naval Observatory, during the same period, for the pay of a few civilian assistants, for labor, and for general expenses, and excluding the the amounts paid for salaries of the six or seven principal astronomers. (See appended Note B.) But it may be objected that this was a sort of expeditionary *tour de force* (though it lasted nearly fifteen years), and that the work of an observatory cannot habitually be kept at such high tension. The Greenwich Observatory offers a standard of comparison which is not open to this objection.

The output of scientific observations from the Greenwich Observatory has certainly been larger and better than it has been at the Washington Observatory in corresponding periods. A comparison between the expenditures of these two observatories is therefore not unfair to the Naval Observatory. In the Appendix to the Greenwich Observations for 1873 (published in 1875) the annual grant to the Royal Observatory for all purposes is stated to be usually about £6,000 (or say $29,200). The Astronomer Royal receives £1,000 per annum ; the chief assistant, from £500 to £600 ; the three assistants next in rank, £320 to £450 ; five assistants of junior grade, £180 to £300. The sum of £600 per annum was expended for the services of computers in the discretion of the Astronomer Royal. "A laborer, a watchman and a gate porter are also employed." It appears that the total resources of the Naval Observatory in the period, 1867 to 1879, excluding pay of superintendent, (which at Greenwich amounts to nearly $5,000), and excluding the pay of line officers on duty at the Observatory as assistants, amounted to an average of $39,875 per annum. This is 36 per cent greater than the corresponding amount for the Greenwich Observatory, and is quite sufficient to allow for the difference in scale of salaries in the two countries, which such services command, as may be seen from the above quoted list. The practical duties for the public service performed by the Greenwich Observatory, such as rating chronometers for the English navy, public time service, and the like, were certainly as great as those performed by the line officers on duty at the Naval Observatory ; and if the value of these services had been subtracted from the Greenwich account as they here are from that of the Washington Observatory, the showing would have been much more unfavorable to the latter.

The account for labor and general services at the Naval Observatory, in comparison with the corresponding account for Greenwich, suggests a promising field for retrenchment. It appears from the appropriation bill for 1882 and subsequent years, that there were employed, one fourth-class clerk, an instrument-maker, two skilled laborers, three watchmen, and seven laborers,—fourteen persons in all, as compared with three for like services at the Greenwich Observatory. •It is probable that a part of this difference is not real—the clerical service at Greenwich coming in as part of the duty of the astronomical service, perhaps, and that for instrumental repairs out of the general contingent fund ; but it is not easy to find the reason for this remarkable disproportion of laborers.

The plans for the new observatory point to the necessity for a very large increase in these forms of expenditure in the future.

Full responsibility for the details of work finally centers upon the man who directs the labors of individual workers — upon the Superintendent of the Arsenal, or Navy yard, of the military post, or of the vessel of war, of the Coast Survey, the Medical bureau, or the astronomical observatory. It is a responsibility which cannot be further delegated or evaded. It can only be exercised with advantage by the man who is professionally conversant with the details of the work. Especially where all, or nearly all, the workers must be men of special professional attainments, is the necessity of professional superintendence more urgent. This statement is so true, and its truth is so universally recognized in ordinary affairs, that the utterance of it, even in this disputed connection, seems like a platitude, for which there would be no excuse but for the fact that its applicability is practically denied in the administration of the Observatory.

SECTION VIII.— Reform Needed in the System of Employment at the Naval Observatory.

The reform really demanded at the Observatory, should go much deeper than the question as to what manner of man ought to be its directing head. The entire system of naval organization is unfavorable to the interests and efficiency of an astronomical establishment. At best not many men can be supported by the Government, or from private endowments, for the purpose of carrying on scientific investigations, even when these concern the every day needs of mankind. It will never be necessary to *impress* into this service the few men who are needed, nor to hold them to it by the bonds of military discipline. The opportunity to engage in scientific work as a profession is something that a few men, here and there, will strive for as other men strive for money or political power. The more responsible posts in scientific work, both theoretical and applied, should be reserved by those who have the power to award them, as the prizes of distinguished merit. This has been the policy of all the great European Governments; and any other tends to restrict the science of a country within provincial limits. There will be no dearth of worthy applicants for scientific positions of any grade, even if the rates of compensation be moderate, provided the

Government arranges efficient and vital organization, and offers a reasonable assurance that promotion shall be based upon the combined claims of zealous industry and the growth of professional attainment. It should be a high honor to occupy a prominent position on the Observatory staff, and it would be so considered under a proper organization.

These principles are violated in the organization of the Naval Observatory. The professors of mathematics designed for duty at the Observatory are commissioned as staff officers in the Navy. They are usually appointed at a time in their professional career (and occasionally before they have any professional experience), when it is impossible to foresee what capacity for independent scientific work of the higher order, they will develop. Yet, once appointed, the technical rank and the actual emolument to which they can attain is rigidly mapped out for the remainder of life in the service. They are beyond the reach of external stimulus. In many cases professional pride will act as an incentive ; if they have the true scientific spirit, the interest of work will sufficiently stimulate, but whether it does or not, the material reward is the same. Those unfortunate divergencies in personal capacity and quality may so operate in the case of two astronomers who are equally earnest, and who may seem to start on an equal footing, in a manner such that one shall quickly mount the ladder of scientific attainment to the highest point, while the other may remain at the foot. It is absurd that the material rewards should be the same.

The arguments which bear upon the system of promotions in the Army and Navy do not apply in a service where so much depends upon a special form of intellectual vigor and capacity. The arguments which advocate a secure tenure of office during efficiency and good behavior cannot, in the case of astronomers, be extended so as to cover promotion for longevity alone. There is no excuse ·for this system as applied in the Observatory, except to found the quibble that the principal astronomers at the Observatory are naval officers.

A great national observatory such as the Naval Observatory is evidently designed to be, should be enabled to draw upon the entire country for the available material in astronomers, which circumstances may render it unable to supply from its own *personnel*. Among the astronomical enterprises which such an observatory should desire to carry on, are some that may require special training and experience of a high order. When such an undertaking is interrupted by the accident of death or resignation of its actual conductor, it will frequently happen that there is no one in the observatory staff able to take up the interrupted work in a proper manner, while it will as frequently happen that exactly the right man for the work can be had elsewhere. Unless the organization of the observatory is such that when the necessity arises new men may be introduced in any grade where it would be most advantageous for the iuterests of the observatory to place them, it will fail in that most essential requisite of a national observatory, the ability to prosecute a prolonged investigation continuously without sensible loss of efficiency at any time. In this respect, the present organization of the Naval Observatory conspicuously fails.

CONCLUSION.

It may seem surprising that a system of organization so manifestly · unsuited to the wants of a scientific institution has endured so long. This is not so much due to the lack of complaint from astronomers, as it is to the manner in which the Observatory has been developed without legislation expressly defining its objects. In a military department, with subordinates subject to order, and transfer of service at will, it is easy to encroach upon the prerogatives of legislation and to build up what are virtually new institutions without express permission from Congress. Such, in great measure, was the early history of the Geological and Geographical Surveys by the Army, as well as of the Army Weather Service. The Army and Navy have facilities which enable them to start such enterprises without attracting much attention They can inaugurate an observatory through the device of building a "house for charts," and stock it with instruments from a general contingent fund for instruments for the Navy. They can then man it with their own officers, requiring no special appropriation at first. Later they can show that the efficiency of the establishment would be increased if a few civilian assistants were allowed ; and thus, from small beginnings, build up an extensive establishment through the power and skill of organization. To be sure, so far as special appropriations may be necessary, Congress, in the act of granting them, does virtually sanction the objects to which they are devoted. But this is a very different thing from the kind of authorization which ought to be accorded to a new enterprise. In granting an appropriation to an existing establishment, the inquiry is usually, not so much whether the institution ought to be supported at all, or whether it is conducted as it ought to be, as it is,—what was the appropriation last year, and why is more wanted this year.

This facility, while it is necessary in operations concerning the military, is pernicious when applied to civil administration. The extension of military control to matters which have no relation to military efficiency is, indeed, highly obnoxious to good government, as Americans regard it. Much evidence exists that Congress looks with disfavor on this form of control in matters which are essentially not military. More than ten years ago the geological and geographical survey in the West, which was conducted by the Army, was taken from that department and consolidated with others to form a civilian bureau. This year the Weather Bureau of the Army Signal Corps has been transferred to civilian management. This transfer grew out of a long-continued agitation in which the investigation of 1884–6, by a joint commission of both Houses of Congress, may be considered to have been the decisive feature. The controversy was precisely of the nature that now exists between astronomers and the naval representatives of the Observatory, except that the arguments for placing the Observatory under technical and civilian control are much more conclusive than in a case like that of the Weather service. The subject-matter of investigation related to details of operation in certain scientific bureaus of Government—to supposed duplication of work and functions—rather than to general principles of administration. Nevertheless, the report of the commission, of which Hon. William B. Allison was chairman, contains some reflections upon the general principles which ought to govern in the conduct of scientific work by the Government. One point upon which the commission appears to have been unanimous is pertinent to the present occasion. This point is very succinctly expressed in the minority report which was signed by Hon. John T. Morgan, Hon. Hilary A. Herbert, and Hon. John T. Tait. They say:

"As a question of proper civil administration, it seems clear to the commission, as appears in the general report, that it is not good government to put a branch of the service that has no necessary relation to military affairs under the regimen of a military establishment and under military organization and command." (Senate Reports, No. 1,285, p. 59; 49th Cong., 1st session.)

On its own account the minority also says:

" It is not consistent with the spirit of our Government that the military should dominate the civil power in any case where such a dangerous course of administration can be avoided." (Ibid., p. 59.)

With the ordinary operations of the Navy Department, astronomers have no more concern than any other class of citizens. They would ordinarily have no more occasion to be exercised over the administration of a depot of charts than those of other professions. But when this " depot " is discovered to be an astronomical observatory, which assumes to represent American astronomy and employs a large staff of professional astronomers in pure scientific investigation, it becomes not only the right but the duty of astronomers to interfere, if, in their judgment, the interests of astronomy and the country require it.

From the account of the early history of the Naval Observatory, it is evident that astronomers did make an effort to secure a proper scientific organization for the Government observatory. There is evidence that this sentiment was alive in 1854, when the Secretary of the Navy in response to an inquiry in regard to the proper name for the observatory wrote:

" It is a Navy affair, and its reputation is the property of the Navy. If it assume another name and character, the next step will be to place a civilian at its head." (Letter of Dec. 12, 1854. See Report of National Academy of Sciences for 1885, p. 64.)

The number of practical astronomers in America in those days was small, and they could exert but a feeble influence. There were few observatories in the land, and, with one exception, they had no independent income. Within the past twenty-five or thirty years there has been a great change in this respect. There are now in the United States nine or ten observatories that are supported from special endowments or from public funds; and in addition to these, a number of university and college observatories where the professors in charge have opportunity to carry on work of investigation in addition to that of instruction. The antagonism to superintendence of the Government observatory by a Naval officer, has, therefore, become more pronounced and aggressive, in proportion to the increase of the astronomical interest in the country. This antagonism has been marked during the past fifteen years, though thus far without evident effect. The distinguished character of many of the superintendents of the Naval Observatory, when it was the practice to detail officers of high rank to that duty, undoubtedly served to restrain the protests of astronomers, though not to silence them. These appointments gave the incumbents shore duty pay at the seat of Government, a comfortable residence, a stable, a garden, and perhaps other desirable perquisites. It is not likely that the public would have applauded what might have been improperly construed as personal attacks upon these distinguished men.

Nevertheless, in 1865 and again in 1867, the earlier administration of the Observatory was sharply criticised by American astronomers of high rank, in articles addressed to the public*. In 1877 naval administration at the Observatory was put on the defensive, as previously shown. In 1882-3 the struggle assumed definite shape and the controversy made some stir in the public press. In 1885, the National Academy of Sciences, in response to a request from the Secretary of the Navy for its opinion in regard to the proposed removal of the Observatory to a new site presented an elaborate report† upon the subject of the organization of the Naval Observatory, in which the present system is arraigned and unequivocally condemned,—urging at the same time in emphatic terms that a change to skilled superintendence be made a condition precedent to the removal. Petitions to like effect have been sent to the Navy Department from various representative educational institutions, such as Harvard College, Johns Hopkins University and others. Outside the Naval Observatory the sentiment of the scientific men of the country is practically unanimous in favor of the change.

*The National Almanac for 1664, by Dr. B. A. Gould; North American Review, Vol. 105 (editorially), by Professor Simon Newcomb, U. S. N.

†See Report of the National Academy for 1885. This report was signed by F. A. P. Barnard, President of Columbia College; A. Graham Bell; J. D. Dana, Professor in Yale College and Editor of the American Journal of Science; S. P. Langley, Director of the Allegheny Observatory (now Secretary of the Smithsonian Institution); Theodore Lyman, E. C. Pickering, Director of the Observatory of Harvard College; and C. A. Young, Director of the Halstead Observatory, Princeton.

Notwithstanding these and many other protests, it has not been possible for astronomers to make much impression upon the authorities of Government in this matter. It 'is difficult for the few astronomers scattered over the country and absorbed in their work, to make effective head against the influences interested in perpetuating the present system at the Observatory. But the justice of their cause will insure their persistence, until some favorable occasion when the authorities of Government choose to examine the question on its merits.

There is no longer any pretense that the new Observatory is not intended to fulfill the functions elsewhere exercised by great national observatories. In 1877, the Superintendent, after reviewing the work at the Observatory, said:

"It will be seen from the foregoing that the observatory is a great national institution, and that within its sphere, it amply returns, both in material value and national fame, all the sums expended upon it." (Report of the Secretary of the Navy for 1877, p. 319.)

Whatever was true in regard to the purely astronomical scope of the Naval Observatory in 1877, will be true in a much greater degree of the new Observatory. So the projectors of the new institution undoubtedly intend, for, otherwise, they would stand convicted of the most unpardonable extravagance.

If confronted with the issue, it is believed that a majority of the officers of the Navy would concede the propriety of turning the Observatory over to those who know how to manage it. It is not surprising that naval officers, who have been or who wish to be detailed to the Naval Observatory, should strive to maintain their hold on that establishment. The duties of officers stationed at the Observatory are not believed to be arduous. It must be pleasant to enjoy the period of shore duty at the capital. It may, therefore, be assumed that the naval officers of the Naval Observatory will never voluntarily relinquish their hold upon it. It appears to be a common belief that even Congress cannot dispossess them, otherwise than by the most explicit legislation.

Naval officers do not need the training which an observatory affords, any more than the clerks in the civil departments do. On this point, the Committee of the National Academy of Sciences, in its report for 1885, well remarks:

"There is already an observatory at Annapolis, but the course of instruction pursued at the naval school there, is of itself evidence how little importance is considered in naval education to attach to the processes of practical astronomy as conducted in fixed observatories. All the astronomical training which the naval cadets receive is confined to the principles of navigation and the use of portable reflecting instruments. It is believed that the observatory of the academy is not used at all, and has not been for many years, and the neglect of it would appear to show that the naval officers stationed there have not the time to occupy themselves with subjects so far outside the necessities of their professional life."

There is, indeed, no reason why naval officers should not furnish time to shipping and rate the chronometers of the Navy. They should be charged with whatever duty is necessary in testing nautical instruments. The connection of these operations with the duties of skilled seamanship is obvious. There seems to be every reason why, following the example of the German, French, Austrian and Italian Governments, our Navy should be provided with a small establishment adequate for this purpose. The necessary expenditure for such purpose need not be a twentieth of that for the new Observatory. If the old observatory, or the observatory at Annapolis be utilized for the purpose, the expense would need to be only a mere trifle, in comparison with the expenditure incurred for the new Observatory. There would be no occasion for the employment of skilled civilian assistants.

It would be of great advantage to the interests of the public service, as well as to those of astronomy, if a change in the form of superintendence of the Government observatory could be made at once and a civilian director appointed. The arrangements making and to be made at the new Observatory at great expenditure, will affect its future efficiency in a marked degree. If they are as wisely made as were those at Pulkowa fifty years ago, or as they are usually made under the direction of competent astronomers, there will be little to alter or regret. If they are made in the manner which experience proves to be the usual rule under unskilled superintendence, it is greatly to be feared that the Government may hereafter be burdened with a cumbersome plant, unsuited to the uses for which it was designed, and costly in its maintenance. For the first twenty years of its existence, the old Observatory was handicapped by the character of its equipment, though money enough had been expended to have supplied essential needs; and for the remainder of its history the arrangements were far from satisfactory, or, indeed, extremely imperfect, if we are to concede the necessity for the expensive alterations now in progress.

In fact, the arrangements for the new Observatory ought not to be carried beyond the most obvious necessities until some settled policy as to scientific work has been formulated by competent authority. One of the ablest American astronomers very pungently says in this connection:

"To build an observatory before knowing what it is going to do is much like designing a machine-shop and putting in a large collection of improved tools and machinery before concluding what the shop is to make, and what are the conditions of the market open to its product." (Professor Newcomb in the North American Review for August, 1881.)

The increasing importance of astronomical science in this country; the rapidly developing intelligence of the general public in scientific matters; and the tendencies of Government in dealing with scientific organizations as illustrated during the past fifteen years in the reorganization of the Geological and the Weather services ; these render it certain that the needed reform cannot be long delayed. This time of removal from the old to the new Observatory is most opportune and appropriate for the change. It is best for all interests that the issue be fairly met and decided now.

The experience of all nations, which have had large astronomical observatories under professional superintendents, demonstrates that the advantages of such a system are not confined to the work of the observatory alone. The observatory becomes an inspiration to astronomical science throughout the land. During recent years our Naval Observtory has stood constantly in an attitude of defense toward astronomers ; while by them it has usually been regarded with a degree of disfavor such as is implied by want of respect for its scientific standing as an institution. It is not natural for any American to rest satisfied that the observatory which is so generously supported by the United States should fail to occupy a commanding position in astronomical science, and to offer a leadership which all astronomers can support with loyalty and pride.

It has been said that science knows no country, and in a certain sense this is true. Science is cosmopolitan in its sympathies. But it is also true that one of the most effective spurs to scientific effort is a strong national pride. The astronomers of other nations are strongly influenced by this sentiment. All astronomers rejoice unreservedly in the triumphs of astronomical research and discovery wherever they are achieved. They are ready to give credit impartially where crdit is due. But every friend of astronomy finds his keenest enjoyment over successes won, in the knowledge that his own country, more than any other, has contributed to win them. It is the National Observatory that must stand as the most conspicuous representative of national astronomy. All Americans would like to feel proud of their National Observatory. Let it, then, be placed in a position where it may be able to assume the leadership that naturally belongs to it.

64

NOTE A.

Extracts from the Report of Hon. Francis Mallory, from the Committee on Naval Affairs, to accompany House Bill, No. 303, in reference to a new house for the Depot of Charts of the Navy. 27th Congress, 2d Session, No. 449. Presented to the House, March 15, 1842.

The following extracts from the essential portions of the Report of Hon. Francis Mallory, from the Committe on Naval Affairs, which served the Navy as authority for organizing and providing for the present Naval Observatory :

" It appears from the statements of its superintendent, that the depot of charts and instruments was established in 1830. The duties at that time required were, the selection, purchase, repairs, and distribution of all the instruments and charts required by the Navy, and to render useful the hydrograpic information which might be contributed by our officers from to time.

"Since its organization, the Navy has not only been furnished with better instruments and more recent charts, at a greatly less original cost than before, but greater care has been observed in their use, consequent upon the regulations of the depot, making the masters of our public vessels directly responsible for each article delivered to them. * * * *

" In the summer of 1838, the honorable Secretary of the Navy, directed the Superintendent to make a constant series of observations in astronomy, magnetism, and meteorology, ordering an additional number of assistants, and granting authority for the purchase of all necessary instruments.

" In the two latter sciences, the observations are made tri-hourly, throughout the day and night, and from year's end to year's end ; and, in the former, the average number of observations is three thousand annually. * * * *

" These observations are intended not only for the benefit of the Navy, but for the country and the world. * * * *

" The house now occupied, and the observatory connected with it, are both private property. The former is inadequate to the purpose for which it is intended, and from its possessing no accommodations for the officers in charge; and the latter is unfit, from its size, and unsafe to the valuable instruments it contains.

" In addition to the saving of money to the Government, and the importance of having our national ships furnished with the most perfect instruments and charts of the most recent surveys, it is unquestionably the fact, that its establishment has disseminated information in the Navy which could scarcely have been attained by other means. The assistants have been obliged, in the pursuance of their duties, to acquire a knowledge of new instruments and new charts, whether they possessed a taste for such pursuits or not—a knolwedge which cannot fail to be useful in the practice of their profession.

" It is proposed to extend its usefulness still further; to make it what it should become in the existing requirements of the naval service."

[The advantages to hydrography are then considered.]

"*Astronomy.*—We are indebted to other nations for the data which enable our ships to cross the ocean. Not only has the Navy failed to contribute to the common stock from which all our navigators borrow, but our country has never yet published an observation of a celestial body, which bore the impress 'by authority;' and it is believed that, until the observations before alluded to in this report, none have ever been directed by the Government which can be considered continuous.

"That great errors exist in the tabulated places of the heavenly bodies, the labors of astronomers of the present day sufficiently prove. Indeed, all who were at all curious in such matters could not have failed to remark how great a difference there was between the observed and computed times of the last annular eclipse visible in the United States.

"Observatories, though not expensive, cannot prosper in our country until we can obtain rest from the pursuit of mercantile affairs, or their charge is undertaken by the Government. The duties are confining; if properly executed, arduous; and but few are qualified by experience or habits to undertake them. If officers can be found with taste for such duties, an observatory will give more information to the world, under a military organization, in one year, than under any other direction in two.

"A small observatory is absolutely essential to the depot; without it the duties cannot be performed. The present tenement was erected at private expense, of slight materials, and is entirely unsuited to the wants of the Navy or the protection of the instruments. From defects in its original construction, a considerable portion of the heavens is entirely obscured to the observer. Nor can these defects be remedied even were the building worthy of alteration; for it is already so frail that its doors have been blown entirely off twice during this winter, leaving the instruments completely exposed to the weather. The Superintendent reports that it is unsafe to continue so much valuable property in such a building longer than the ensuing spring. The value of the instruments and charts under his charge, is never less than $60,000, and will be greatly increased within a short time."

"*Magnetism.*—This subject is scarcely less important to the Navy than astronomy. Without a knowledge of the variation of the compass, none but coasting craft dare venture beyond the precincts of a harbor; yet how few have more than a practical knowledge of the mode of determining its amount. * * *

"The magnetic observatories which were established by the European Governments two years since, and which have a location in almost every part of the world, were earnestly recommended to us by the learned men of England. * * *

"Whatever these results may be, the Navy is deeply interested in them, more so than any other branch of society; and shall it be said that we have appropriated the hard-earned labors of others to benefit our Navy without compelling it to bear its portion ? "

"*Meteorology.*— To be a good judge of the weather is considered an important qualification for a seaman; the safety of a ship and her crew may depend on the promptness and accuracy of his judgment. Meteorology has been more generally pursued in the United States than any other of the physical sciences. * * * Meteorological observations are more important at night than by day, because of their scarcity hitherto; and it is scarcely to be expected that amateurs can be found in sufficient numbers to make all the required observations.

Night watching in stormy weather finds few followers, and we can only hope to obtain the desired information, when those engaged in its pursuits have *duty* to compel a flagging inclination.

"Deeming an establishment of this description essential to the welfare of the Navy, the committee report the accompanying bill."

NOTE.— This bill did not, however, pass. The bill which did pass, originated in the Senate, but was identical in terms with that which the Committee on Naval Affairs reported in the House with the foregoing recommendation.

NOTE B.

AVAILABLE RESOURCES OF THE NAVAL OBSERVATORY SINCE JULY 1, 1867.

The greater part of the employees at the Naval Observatory hold commissions in the Navy, and their salaries and allowances are paid from the general appropriation. Nothing short of a careful computation from the records of the Navy and Treasury Departments would serve to furnish an accurate account of expenditures for the Observatory. In lieu of this it is believed that fairly good estimates can be derived from consultation of the reports of the Observatory and the Navy Register as to *personnel*, together with the direct annual appropriations for the support of the Observatory.

In order to get a clear view of the current operating expenses of the Observatory, it will be necessary to subtract certain items found in the appropriation bills. Congress made large appropriations for observing the Transits of Venus in 1874 and 1882, which were expended by a commission representing several scientific bureaus of Government. These have no connection with Observatory appropriations, and may be regarded as chargeable to national astronomy at large. But some small incidental appropriations for the Transit of Venus operations were included in the appropriations for the Observatory. Consistency requires that these should be excluded from the account of current expenses. Following are the items excluded, in order to ascertain the regular operating expenses of the Observatory.

Great Telescope and its tower, etc., 1870–1874.	$67,000
Incidental Transit of Venus, as explained, 1871–1884,	16,950
For account of Hall's second Arctic Expedition........	5,000
Watchman for the new observatory to July.1, 1891...	6,480
New observatory to July 1, 1891......................	475,000

Total of incidental and extraordinary expenses 1870–1891..	$570,430

The account of expenses here considered begins with July 1, 1867, and ends with June 30, 1891. After the revival of astronomy in 1861 and previous to 1867 the Observatory may be regarded as having been under the management of astronomers. Previous to 1867, also, the Observatory was charged with the care of charts. The total current expenses of the Naval Observatory during the period, 1861 to 1867 were less than they have been at any time since.

Direct Appropriations for Civilian Assistants, Labor and General Expenses, Including Deficiencies.

Fiscal Year.	Amount.	Fiscal Year.	Amount.	Fiscal Year.	Amount.
1867-8	$21,500	1875-6	$17,500	1883-4	$26,138
1868-9	16,600	1876-7	21,300	1884-5	26,436
1869-70	19,000	1877-8	21,000	1885-6	26,336
1870-1	19,800	1878-9	22,100	1886-7	26,736
1871-2	22,300	1879-80	25,786	1887-8	26,136
1872-3	24,200	1880-1	24,537	1888-9	27,336
1873-4	23,100	1881-2	26,936	1889-90	29,136
1874-5	19,050	1882-3	28,764	1890-1	29,050

The reports of the Observatory do not always show the precise dates when newly appointed professors reported for duty, nor the exact dates when others resigned, were transferred to other duty, or were retired. Notwithstanding this difficulty the average number of professors on duty in any given period and their compensation, exclusive of allowances, can be stated with sufficient accuracy for the purposes of this exhibit. This does not include the pay of professors in retirement. The part of this item which belongs to the Observatory account amounts to many thousand dollars.

For brevity and convenience, the entire period under consideration will be divided into four periods of six years each. In connection with each is given the average number of professors on duty at the Observatory in that period; the average compensation which that corps received at the Observatory; the average of direct appropriations for the same interval, taken from the foregoing table; and the total, which may be considered as the total income of the Observatory, exclusive of the amounts paid to officers of the line for salaries.

PERIOD.	No. Professors.	Average Pay of Professors.	Average Direct Appropriation.	For Professors and General Expenses.
1867-1873	7	$16,010	$20,567	$36,580
1873-1879	8	22,500	20,675	43,170
1879-1885	5	14,610	26,433	41,040
1885-1891	5	15,890	27,455	43,340

For reasons already stated, it is still more difficult to ascertain the exact terms of service of officers of the naval line at the Observatory with the exact amount of compensation received by them. A rough estimate of averages can be made, however, which will probably be found to be not far from the truth. The following table exhibits for each of the adopted periods, the average number of line officers on duty at the Observatory, including the Superintendent; the average compensation received by them for such service, roughly estimated; and the average of the total annual expenses for current operating purposes in the respective periods:

PERIOD.	No. Line Officers.	Average Pay of Line Officers.	Total Annual Resources of the Observatory.
1867–1873	4	$10,400	$47,000
1873–1879	5	12,800	56,000
1879–1885	9	19,500	60,500
1885–1891	10	17,500	60,800

Assembling the separate items, it appears that from June 30, 1867, to July 1, 1891, there has been expended for the Observatory on account of current expenses about $1,346,000; and for extraordinary expenses, not including appropriations on account of the Transits of Venus, which should not be considered chargeable to the Observatory alone, a total of $548,480. For the current fiscal year the appropriation for the new Observatory is $136,689, and for current maintenance the expenditures will probably reach $66,000. This gives an estimated total expenditure for all purposes in relation to the Naval Observatory during the twenty-five years following June 30, 1867, of very nearly $2,100,000, or about $84,000 per annum.

Assuming that the existence of the Naval Observatory has made no difference in the number of officers of the line of the Navy that would have been employed by the Government, and deducting the amount of salary paid to them, the total charge for current expenses has been about $985,000 during the twenty-four years. Including the present fiscal year, and adding the amounts for extraordinary expenditures, as before, the total for twenty-five years is about $1,720,000, or not far from $69,000 per annum—when the pay of line officers is left out of the account.